MARGARET THATCHER

MARGARET THATCHER

Bernard Garfinkel

CHELSEA HOUSE PUBLISHERS
NEW YORK

MANAGING EDITOR: William P. Hansen
ASSOCIATE EDITOR: John Haney
CONSULTANT: Mark Sufrin
EDITORIAL STAFF: Linda Cuckovich
Susan Quist
Katherine Melchior
ART DIRECTOR: Susan Lusk
LAYOUT: Irene Friedman
COVER DESIGN: Peterson Design
PICTURE RESEARCH: Joanna Wissinger

5 7 9 8 6

Library of Congress Cataloging in Publications Data

Garfinkel, Bernard Max. MARGARET THATCHER

(World leaders past and present)
Bibliography: p
Includes index
Summary: A biography of Great Britain's first woman prime minister.

1. Thatcher, Margaret—Juvenile literature.

2. Great Britain—Politics and government—1964–1979 Juvenile literature.

3. Great Britain—Politics and government—1979—Juvenile literature.

4. Prime ministers—Great Britain—Biography—Juvenile literature.

Thatcher, Margaret. 2. Prime ministers
I. Title. II. Series.
DA591.T47G38 1984 941.085'8'0924 [B] [92] 84-15554

ISBN 0-87754-552-9
    0-7910-0603-4 (pbk.)

Contents

JOHN ADAMS
JOHN QUINCY ADAMS
KONRAD ADENAUER
ALEXANDER THE GREAT
SALVADOR ALLENDE
MARC ANTONY
CORAZON AQUINO
YASIR ARAFAT
KING ARTHUR
HAFEZ AL-ASSAD
KEMAL ATATÜRK
ATTILA
CLEMENT ATTLEE
AUGUSTUS CAESAR
MENACHEM BEGIN
DAVID BEN-GURION
OTTO VON BISMARCK
LÉON BLUM
SIMON BOLÍVAR
CESARE BORGIA
WILLY BRANDT
LEONID BREZHNEV
JULIUS CAESAR
JOHN CALVIN
JIMMY CARTER
FIDEL CASTRO
CATHERINE THE GREAT
CHARLEMAGNE
CHIANG KAI-SHEK
WINSTON CHURCHILL
GEORGES CLEMENCEAU
CLEOPATRA
CONSTANTINE THE GREAT
HERNÁN CORTÉS
OLIVER CROMWELL
GEORGES-JACQUES
   DANTON
JEFFERSON DAVIS
MOSHE DAYAN
CHARLES DE GAULLE
EAMON DE VALERA
EUGENE DEBS
DENG XIAOPING
BENJAMIN DISRAELI
ALEXANDER DUBČEK
FRANÇOIS & JEAN-CLAUDE
   DUVALIER
DWIGHT EISENHOWER
ELEANOR OF AQUITAINE
ELIZABETH I
FAISAL
FERDINAND & ISABELLA
FRANCISCO FRANCO
BENJAMIN FRANKLIN

FREDERICK THE GREAT
INDIRA GANDHI
MOHANDAS GANDHI
GIUSEPPE GARIBALDI
AMIN & BASHIR GEMAYEL
GENGHIS KHAN
WILLIAM GLADSTONE
MIKHAIL GORBACHEV
ULYSSES S. GRANT
ERNESTO "CHE" GUEVARA
TENZIN GYATSO
ALEXANDER HAMILTON
DAG HAMMARSKJÖLD
HENRY VIII
HENRY OF NAVARRE
PAUL VON HINDENBURG
HIROHITO
ADOLF HITLER
HO CHI MINH
KING HUSSEIN
IVAN THE TERRIBLE
ANDREW JACKSON
JAMES I
WOJCIECH JARUZELSKI
THOMAS JEFFERSON
JOAN OF ARC
POPE JOHN XXIII
POPE JOHN PAUL II
LYNDON JOHNSON
BENITO JUÁREZ
JOHN KENNEDY
ROBERT KENNEDY
JOMO KENYATTA
AYATOLLAH KHOMEINI
NIKITA KHRUSHCHEV
KIM IL SUNG
MARTIN LUTHER KING, JR.
HENRY KISSINGER
KUBLAI KHAN
LAFAYETTE
ROBERT E. LEE
VLADIMIR LENIN
ABRAHAM LINCOLN
DAVID LLOYD GEORGE
LOUIS XIV
MARTIN LUTHER
JUDAS MACCABEUS
JAMES MADISON
NELSON & WINNIE
   MANDELA
MAO ZEDONG
FERDINAND MARCOS
GEORGE MARSHALL

MARY, QUEEN OF SCOTS
TOMÁŠ MASARYK
GOLDA MEIR
KLEMENS VON METTERNICH
JAMES MONROE
HOSNI MUBARAK
ROBERT MUGABE
BENITO MUSSOLINI
NAPOLÉON BONAPARTE
GAMAL ABDEL NASSER
JAWAHARLAL NEHRU
NERO
NICHOLAS II
RICHARD NIXON
KWAME NKRUMAH
DANIEL ORTEGA
MOHAMMED REZA PAHLAVI
THOMAS PAINE
CHARLES STEWART
   PARNELL
PERICLES
JUAN PERÓN
PETER THE GREAT
POL POT
MUAMMAR EL-QADDAFI
RONALD REAGAN
CARDINAL RICHELIEU
MAXIMILIEN ROBESPIERRE
ELEANOR ROOSEVELT
FRANKLIN ROOSEVELT
THEODORE ROOSEVELT
ANWAR SADAT
HAILE SELASSIE
PRINCE SIHANOUK
JAN SMUTS
JOSEPH STALIN
SUKARNO
SUN YAT-SEN
TAMERLANE
MOTHER TERESA
MARGARET THATCHER
JOSIP BROZ TITO
TOUSSAINT L'OUVERTURE
LEON TROTSKY
PIERRE TRUDEAU
HARRY TRUMAN
QUEEN VICTORIA
LECH WALESA
GEORGE WASHINGTON
CHAIM WEIZMANN
WOODROW WILSON
XERXES
EMILIANO ZAPATA
ZHOU ENLAI

CHELSEA HOUSE PUBLISHERS

ON LEADERSHIP
Arthur M. Schlesinger, jr.

LEADERSHIP, it may be said, is really what makes the world go round. Love no doubt smooths the passage; but love is a private transaction between consenting adults. Leadership is a public transaction with history. The idea of leadership affirms the capacity of individuals to move, inspire and mobilize masses of people so that they act together in pursuit of an end. Sometimes leadership serves good purposes, sometimes bad; but whether the end is benign or evil, great leaders are those men and women who leave their personal stamp on history.

Now, the very concept of leadership implies the proposition that individuals can make a difference. This proposition has never been universally accepted. From classical times to the present day, eminent thinkers have regarded individuals as no more than the agents and pawns of larger forces, whether the gods and goddesses of the ancient world or, in the modern era, race, class, nation, the dialectic, the will of the people, the spirit of the times, history itself. Against such forces, the individual dwindles into insignificance.

So contends the thesis of historical determinism. Tolstoy's great novel *War and Peace* offers a famous statement of the case. Why, Tolstoy asked, did millions of men in the Napoleonic wars, denying their human feelings and their common sense, move back and forth across Europe slaughtering their fellows? "The war," Tolstoy answered, "was bound to happen simply because it was bound to happen." All prior history predetermined it. As for leaders, they, Tolstoy said, "are but the labels that serve to give a name to an end and, like labels, they have the least possible connection with the event." The greater the leader, "the more conspicuous the inevitability and the predestination of every act he commits." The leader, said Tolstoy, is "the slave of history."

Determinism takes many forms. Marxism is the determinism of class, Nazism the determinism of race. But the idea of men and women as the slaves of history runs athwart the deepest human instincts. Rigid determinism abolishes the idea of human freedom—the assumption of free choice that underlies every move we make, every word we speak, every thought we think. It abolishes the idea of human responsibility, since it is manifestly unfair to reward or punish people for actions that are by definition beyond their control. No one can live consistently by any deterministic creed. The Marxist states prove this themselves by their extreme susceptibility to the cult of leadership.

More than that, history refutes the idea that individuals make no difference. In December 1931 a British politician crossing Park Avenue in New York City between 76th and 77th Streets around ten-thirty at night looked in the wrong direction and was knocked down by an automobile—a moment, he later recalled, of a man aghast, a world aglare: "I do not understand why I was not broken like an eggshell or squashed like a gooseberry." Fourteen months later an American politician, sitting in an open car in Miami, Florida, was fired on by an assassin; the man beside him was hit. Those who believe that individuals make no difference to history might well ponder whether the next two decades would have been the same had Mario Contasini's car killed Winston Churchill in 1931 and Giuseppe Zangara's bullet killed Franklin Roosevelt in 1933. Suppose, in addition, that Adolf Hitler had been killed in the street fighting during the Munich *Putsch* of 1923 and that Lenin had died of typhus during the First World War. What would the 20th century be like now?

For better or for worse, individuals do make a difference. "The notion that a people can run itself and its affairs anonymously," wrote the philosopher William James, "is now well known to be the silliest of absurdities. Mankind does nothing save through initiatives on the part of inventors, great or small, and imitation by the rest of us—these are the sole factors in human progress. Individuals of genius show the way, and set the patterns, which common people then adopt and follow."

Leadership, James suggests, means leadership in thought as well as in action. In the long run, leaders in thought may well make the greater difference to the world. But, as Woodrow Wilson once said, "Those only are leaders of men, in the general eye, who lead in action. . . . It is at their hands that new thought gets its translation into the crude language of deeds." Leaders in thought often invent in solitude and obscurity, leaving to later generations the tasks of imitation. Leaders in action—the leaders portrayed in this series—have to be effective in their own time.

And they cannot be effective by themselves. They must act in response to the rhythms of their age. Their genius must be adapted, in a phrase of William James's, "to the receptivities of the moment." Leaders are useless without followers. "There goes the mob," said the French politician hearing a clamor in the streets. "I am their leader. I must follow them." Great leaders turn the inchoate emotions of the mob to purposes of their own. They seize on the opportunities of their time, the hopes, fears, frustrations, crises, potentialities.

8

They succeed when events have prepared the way for them, when the community is waiting to be aroused, when they can provide the clarifying and organizing ideas. Leadership ignites the circuit between the individual and the mass and thereby alters history.

It may alter history for better or for worse. Leaders have been responsible for the most extravagant follies and most monstrous crimes that have beset suffering humanity. They have also been vital in such gains as humanity has made in individual freedom, religious and racial tolerance, social justice and respect for human rights.

There is no sure way to tell in advance who is going to lead for good and who for evil. But a glance at the gallery of men and women in *World Leaders—Past and Present* suggests some useful tests.

One test is this: do leaders lead by force or by persuasion? By command or by consent? Through most of history leadership was exercised by the divine right of authority. The duty of followers was to defer and to obey. "Theirs not to reason why,/ Theirs but to do and die." On occasion, as with the so-called "enlightened despots" of the 18th century in Europe, absolutist leadership was animated by humane purposes. More often, absolutism nourished the passion for domination, land, gold and conquest and resulted in tyranny.

The great revolution of modern times has been the revolution of equality. The idea that all people should be equal in their legal condition has undermined the old structures of authority, hierarchy and deference. The revolution of equality has had two contrary effects on the nature of leadership. For equality, as Alexis de Tocqueville pointed out in his great study *Democracy in America*, might mean equality in servitude as well as equality in freedom.

"I know of only two methods of establishing equality in the political world," Tocqueville wrote. "Rights must be given to every citizen, or none at all to anyone . . . save one, who is the master of all." There was no middle ground "between the sovereignty of all and the absolute power of one man." In his astonishing prediction of 20th-century totalitarian dictatorship, Tocqueville explained how the revolution of equality could lead to the *"Führerprinzip"* and more terrible absolutism than the world had ever known.

But when rights are given to every citizen and the sovereignty of all is established, the problem of leadership takes a new form, becomes more exacting than ever before. It is easy to issue commands and enforce them by the rope and the stake, the concentration camp and the *gulag*. It is much harder to use argument and achievement to overcome opposition and win consent. The Founding Fathers of the United States understood the difficulty. They believed that history had given them the opportunity to decide, as

Alexander Hamilton wrote in the first Federalist Paper, whether men are indeed capable of basing government on "reflection and choice, or whether they are forever destined to depend . . . on accident and force."

Government by reflection and choice called for a new style of leadership and a new quality of followership. It required leaders to be responsive to popular concerns, and it required followers to be active and informed participants in the process. Democracy does not eliminate emotion from politics; sometimes it fosters demagoguery; but it is confident that, as the greatest of democratic leaders put it, you cannot fool all of the people all of the time. It measures leadership by results and retires those who overreach or falter or fail.

It is true that in the long run despots are measured by results too. But they can postpone the day of judgment, sometimes indefinitely, and in the meantime they can do infinite harm. It is also true that democracy is no guarantee of virtue and intelligence in government, for the voice of the people is not necessarily the voice of God. But democracy, by assuring the rights of opposition, offers built-in resistance to the evils inherent in absolutism. As the theologian Reinhold Niebuhr summed it up, "Man's capacity for justice makes democracy possible, but man's inclination to injustice makes democracy necessary."

A second test for leadership is the end for which power is sought. When leaders have as their goal the supremacy of a master race or the promotion of totalitarian revolution or the acquisition and exploitation of colonies or the protection of greed and privilege or the preservation of personal power, it is likely that their leadership will do little to advance the cause of humanity. When their goal is the abolition of slavery, the liberation of women, the enlargement of opportunity for the poor and powerless, the extension of equal rights to racial minorities, the defense of the freedoms of expression and opposition, it is likely that their leadership will increase the sum of human liberty and welfare.

Leaders have done great harm to the world. They have also conferred great benefits. You will find both sorts in this series. Even "good" leaders must be regarded with a certain wariness. Leaders are not demigods; they put on their trousers one leg after another just like ordinary mortals. No leader is infallible, and every leader needs to be reminded of this at regular intervals. Irreverence irritates leaders but is their salvation. Unquestioning submission corrupts leaders and demeans followers. Making a cult of a leader is always a mistake. Fortunately hero worship generates its own antidote. "Every hero," said Emerson, "becomes a bore at last."

The signal benefit the great leaders confer is to embolden the rest of us to live according to our own best selves, to be active, insistent, and resolute in affirming our own sense of things. For great leaders attest to the reality of human freedom against the supposed inevitabilities of history. And they attest to the wisdom and power that may lie within the most unlikely of us, which is why Abraham Lincoln remains the supreme example of great leadership. A great leader, said Emerson, exhibits new possibilities to all humanity. "We feed on genius. . . . Great men exist that there may be greater men."

Great leaders, in short, justify themselves by emancipating and empowering their followers. So humanity struggles to master its destiny, remembering with Alexis de Tocqueville: "It is true that around every man a fatal circle is traced beyond which he cannot pass; but within the wide verge of that circle he is powerful and free; as it is with man, so with communities."

—*New York*

1

"Resign, Resign"

Margaret Thatcher, the prime minister of Great Britain, walked quickly into the House of Commons. The assembled members grew quiet. It was April 3, 1982, and the British parliament was meeting in its first emergency session in more than 25 years.

The reason for urgency was obvious. The day before, without advance warning, Argentina had invaded and conquered the Falkland Islands, one of Britain's last overseas territories.

The Falklands, which Argentina calls the Malvinas, are a tiny group of islands in the south Atlantic near the tip of South America. Treeless and wind-swept, they have been under British control since 1833. The 1,800 loyal British subjects now on the islands endure rain, fog, and cold to live a poor and simple life. Mainly, they occupy themselves with raising the 650,000 sheep that are the islands' major industry. The Falklands' most numerous other inhabitants are penguins—some 10 million of them.

Such a place hardly seems like an inviting target for an invasion. But Argentina insisted that the Falkland Islands belonged to it and that Britain

---

Demonstrators in Scotland protest Mrs. Thatcher's economic policies. Three million Britons were out of work at the time of the crisis in the Falklands.

April 2, 1982: Argentine
marines raise their na-
tional flag at Port Stanley
in the Falkland Islands.

had seized them illegally. The two countries had been trying to settle this argument by talking for the past 15 years. But they had made little progress. Now Argentina had suddenly substituted force for talk, and Britain was the loser.

In the House of Commons Margaret Thatcher began to speak, offering her government's defense against her critics. There had been no warning or intelligence reports to suggest that the attack would take place. Also, there had been no way to get a British military force to such a remote place quickly enough to stop the Argentines from taking the islands.

"Resign, resign," some members shouted. The cries came not just from opposition Labor Party members but from members of her own Conservative Party as well. One by one, Labor Party members expressed their rage and their belief that Britain's shame was the fault of the government—and its leader, Margaret Thatcher.

The Labor Party's deputy leader, Dennis Healy, pressed the attack. Britain, he said, had been

Mrs. Thatcher aboard the British nuclear submarine HMS *Resolution*. Her commitment to Britain's nuclear forces led to criticism early in the Falklands crisis. Some M.P.s and military chiefs complained that concentrating on nuclear forces had left Britain with insufficient conventional capabilities.

"caught with its pants down." Margaret Thatcher had "crippled the Royal Navy" by reducing the number of fighting ships in order to pay for a $13 billion Trident nuclear submarine program that was of no use in a crisis such as this.

Prime Minister Thatcher was clearly at a disadvantage. There was little she could say in her defense. Usually she enjoyed the tough verbal combat of parliamentary debate—with good reason. She had a quick mind and a quicker tongue. She had enormous self-confidence, she liked a fight, and she liked to win.

But today Margaret Thatcher stood accused of letting her country down. It was surely the worst moment she had experienced in the nearly three years since she had become Britain's first woman prime minister. And the Falklands disaster came on top of a recent poll that showed public approval of her performance had fallen to a new low of just 25%. No British leader in recent times had been so unpopular.

When Margaret Thatcher took office in the spring of 1979, she had promised to put the British economy back on its feet. Her economic program, she said, would reduce inflation, break the power of unions to disrupt the economy, create new industry and trade, and bring the country to a new level of prosperity.

And she had promised even more: to bring about a complete and radical change in British society. This she would do by dismantling the welfare state— the network of government-sponsored social programs that had been expanding in Britain since the end of World War II.

She believed in a free economy, not in state control. The welfare state, she argued, destroyed people's self-reliance and initiative. It showered them with benefits that made them lazy. It controlled the economy, regulated people's lives, and reduced freedom. "There can be no liberty without economic liberty," she once said.

During her three years in office, however, she had not been able to change the welfare state very much. And prosperity was nowhere in sight. Brit-

British paratrooper escorting young Argentine POW, near Port San Carlos in the Falkland Islands. British troops were generally older and better trained than the young conscripts in the Argentine army.

British Royal Marines departing for the Falklands aboard the assault ship HMS *Fearless* in April 1982.

May 12, 1982: Troops line the rails of the luxury liner *Queen Elizabeth 2*, requisitioned by the British navy as a military transport during the Falklands crisis.

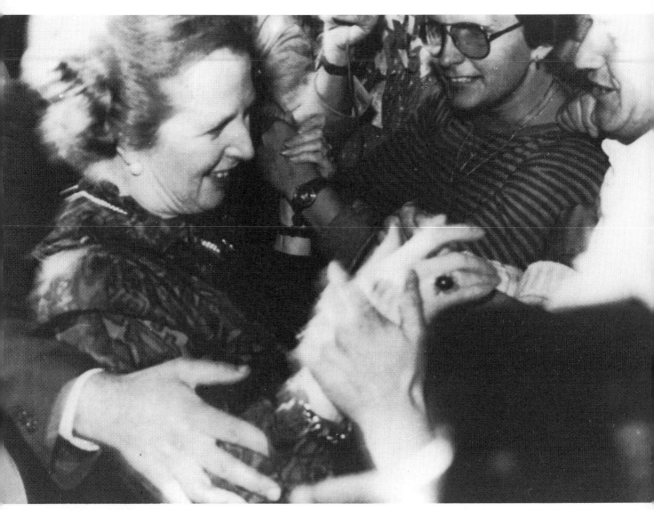

Mrs. Thatcher greeted by
well-wishers outside 10
Downing Street, her offi-
cial London residence, after announcing the Argen-
tine surrender.

ain now had an unemployment rate of 12.5%. That meant that more than 3 million of the country's 26 million workers had no jobs. At the same time, more and more companies were failing and declaring bankruptcy, unable to pay their business debts.

Many in her own party were losing their faith in her, saying that her economic program would never work. Some even felt that it would destroy the British economy and, in fact, Britain as well. They urged her to change course.

A less determined person might have given up, might have lost faith in her ideals and confidence in her ability to reach her goal. But Margaret Thatcher gave no sign that she would buckle under pressure.

Now, in April 1982, she faced a difficult task: to challenge an act of aggression that had taken place 8,000 miles away from Great Britain in a stormy corner of the Atlantic. She met the problem head on.

Prime Minister Thatcher sent out a fleet of 98 ships carrying 8,000 fighting men to take the Falklands back. There was, she believed, a principle involved: aggression must not be tolerated. And she believed it was a principle worth fighting for.

When she was asked what would happen if the mission failed, she replied, "Failure? The possibilities do not exist."

Seventy-four days later, a British commander accepted the surrender of the Argentine troops in the Falklands.

Margaret Thatcher's popularity soared. She had given Britain back its pride. "We knew what we had to do and we went about it and did it," she said. "Great Britain is great again."

Many Britons agreed, more than enough to give her an overwhelming victory when she ran again for prime minister in June 1983. In the face of her fame and popularity, it was hard to believe that just eight years before, she was an untried, almost unknown politician, an outsider who somehow had crashed the party's inner circle, a grocer's daughter from a small town named Grantham, 120 miles north of London.

I never had any doubts about our armed forces. I knew it would be difficult, but I knew they could do it.
—MARGARET THATCHER
after British forces recaptured the Falkland Islands

British marines raise the Union Jack near Port San Carlos in the Falklands.

ROBERTS North Par

LIVE for extra flavour!

NORTH
POST OFFICE

HOGG

Giro

VOTE
HOGG

MARGARET THATCHER
Leader of the Conservative Party

2

Grocer's Daughter

In Grantham, a Midlands town with a population of about 30,000 people, where Margaret Hilda Roberts was born in 1926, she is remembered as a very earnest and serious-minded girl. She may not have thought of life as a business as she grew up, but she certainly liked to do her level best at everything she tried. Even as a young girl she loved to win, and she was not shy about insisting on her self-worth. When she was nine years old, she won a poetry-reading contest at her elementary school. Congratulating her, the school's headmistress said, "You were lucky to win." "I wasn't lucky," Margaret replied. "I deserved it."

Her father, Alfred Roberts, had a family grocery store which also served as the local post office. A public-spirited man, he took an active part in the civic life of Grantham. He was a member of the town council for 25 years, and in 1945 he served a one-year term as mayor.

Margaret and her sister, Muriel, who was four years older, grew up in an apartment over the store. Her mother, Beatrice, helped her father in the store, and when Margaret and Muriel were teenagers, they also lent a hand.

Newlyweds Margaret Roberts and businessman Denis Thatcher in 1951. Mr. Thatcher was a successful director of his family's paint business.

The grocery store owned by Mrs. Thatcher's father in Grantham, England. Margaret grew up in the apartment above the store.

At Kesteven Grammar School in Grantham, to which she won a scholarship, she took elocution lessons. She also played hockey so well that she became the youngest captain the school team ever had. Studious and competitive, she did well enough to be accepted at Oxford, one of the world's great-

est and most prestigious universities.

Alfred Roberts believed strongly in education, though few girls from Grantham ever went to a university, much less Oxford. She needed Latin to enter Oxford, but her grammar school had not offered the language. Her father paid for a Latin

Oxford University in Oxford, England. One of the oldest universities in Europe, Oxford is internationally renowned and maintains high academic entrance requirements, accepting only the most outstanding applicants from British high schools. Margaret did exceptionally well to gain a place there in 1944, since not until the 1970s did Oxford begin admitting substantial numbers of applicants from the working class.

Queen Elizabeth II, enthroned in the House of Lords at a State Opening of Parliament, addresses the assembled members of the House of Lords and the House of Commons. There remains a place for pageantry in British politics even in modern times.

> I'm a romantic at heart. There are times when I get home at night, and everything has got on top of me, when I shed a few tears silently, alone.
> —MARGARET THATCHER

tutor so that Margaret could meet the entrance requirement.

She was already interested in politics, but at Oxford she studied chemistry because it would make getting a job easier. At the same time, she joined the Oxford University Conservative Association and became its chairman. Ironically, she was not allowed to take part in the debates of the Oxford Union. The Union was the school's most famous debating forum, where many politicians before her had polished their speechmaking skills. But the Union did not admit women as members until 1963.

When she graduated in 1947, she went to work as a research chemist at a plastics manufacturing company in Essex. There she began to attend gatherings of the local Conservative Party. In 1950 the party selected her as the candidate to run for a seat in the House of Commons from Dartford. This was a "safe" Labor Party seat (one with a strong Labor majority). She had no chance of winning. She would be running just for the exercise, but with the knowledge that this was traditional for beginning politicians.

Mrs. Thatcher, newly elected Conservative M.P. for Finchley, with her children, Mark and Carol, in 1959.

Harold Macmillan, the Conservative premier who made Margaret Thatcher a junior minister in Britain's Ministry of Pensions and National Insurance in 1962. The new position gave Thatcher her first experience of presenting legislation to parliament.

She was 23 that year, the youngest woman candidate in Great Britain. She lost the election but impressed the local Conservative Party regulars. They liked her personality and admired the hard work she put in during long evenings of electioneering after working all day at the plastics plant. In 1951 she ran for the Dartford seat again and lost again, though by fewer votes.

During the 1950 campaign she had met Denis Thatcher, a businessman who was 10 years older than she and divorced. Their friendship blossomed, and they were married in 1951. Two years later she gave birth to twins, a boy and a girl, Mark and Carol. She had begun to study law in 1950, and four months after the twins were born, she qualified as a barrister. Her specialties were tax and patent law, and she practiced until 1959.

In that year, she got what she had wanted most, a chance to run for a safe Conservative seat in the House of Commons, which, with the House of Lords, forms Britain's parliament. She won easily and became the House of Commons member representing Finchley, an affluent suburb north of London.

The twins were now in boarding school. Her husband was on his way to achieving substantial success in the paint business. She was now ready to devote herself to the political career she had always wanted.

Her prospects for a rapid climb up the parliamentary ladder did not seem outstanding. She was neither well-known nor a member of the Conservative Party establishment, the inner circle that controlled its policies. This meant that she had no powerful friends backing her. But in fact her rise was quite rapid. Soon after she took her seat in the Commons, she introduced her first bill, guaranteeing the press and the public the right to attend meetings of local government councils. She was prompted to do this after a number of councils controlled by Labor Party members refused to admit reporters from anti-union newspapers.

The bill was an early version of the "sunshine laws" that have been passed in the United States to prevent government agencies and legislative committees from meeting in secret. Thatcher's choice of this bill proved to be a shrewd move. It attracted attention as an important piece of legislation. Learning the parliamentary ropes as she went along, she negotiated and fought for the bill. It became law on June 1, 1961.

Margaret Thatcher had demonstrated again her confidence and self-assurance. As she said later, "Since I first stood for parliament in 1950, when I was 23, I haven't doubted that I could cope with whatever I was doing."

In short order, she had succeeded in bringing herself to the attention of Conservative Party leaders. In 1962, when a vacancy occurred in the Ministry of Pensions and National Insurance, Conservative Prime Minister Harold Macmillan made her a junior minister. Often she presented legislation for the ministry in the House. This involved convincing members that the legislation was needed. In doing so, she discovered how much she liked a

I'm a born hard worker. I watched my mother work like a Trojan in the shop and home.
—MARGARET THATCHER

Margaret Thatcher in 1971
with children at the American School in London.
Praised as a "fast learner"
by her colleagues, she
quickly mastered all as-
pects of the administration
of British education.

good argument with an opposing member.

She had to give up her junior ministry in 1964 when the Conservative Party lost the election. But with the Conservatives in opposition, she was promoted from the back bench, where junior members sit, to the front bench, where party leaders and senior members sit. Here she took an active part in presenting party positions during debates.

Traditionally in the House of Commons, when a party is out of power it appoints a shadow cabinet whose members, from the prime minister on down, correspond to the members of the governing party's cabinet. The Conservative Party was out of power for six years, until Edward Heath led it to victory in 1970. During that time Margaret Thatcher held a number of front bench appointments. She served as the junior front bench spokesperson for pensions and national insurance, and then for treasury matters. She became a member of the shadow

Margaret Thatcher, Britain's new secretary of state for education and science, in the garden of 10 Downing Street in 1970 with Prime Minister Edward Heath (left) and the lord chancellor, Quintin Hogg.

cabinet in 1967 as the chief spokesperson for electric power. In 1968 she became the chief spokesperson for transport, and a year later, the shadow minister for education. By 1970 she was recognized as one of the leading Conservative speakers in the House. She also gained a reputation as a "quick learner" who could rapidly master a new subject— and then perform well in presenting and defending it from the front bench.

In the election of June 1970, Edward Heath, who had been leader of the party since 1965, led the Conservatives to victory over Harold Wilson and the Labor Party. Running for reelection to her seat in Finchley, Margaret Thatcher increased her majority to nearly two to one over her opponent.

On June 28, when Heath announced his new cabinet, Margaret Thatcher was named minister of education and science. She was the only woman in the cabinet. Now, for the first time, she would have the opportunity to exercise power as a member of the government.

Her feelings about education grew out of her own experience, as well as her basic conservative philosophy. She believed strongly in education, but she was against too much government control over it. Previous Labor governments had set down strict guidelines that local school authorities had to follow. Margaret Thatcher immediately moved to reverse this trend.

Local authorities, she said, should be free to decide the kind of secondary schools they wanted and the kind of programs the schools would offer. But decisions should be made only after the school authorities found out what parents and teachers wanted. The main goal, she insisted, was to make sure that children had the opportunity to get an education that was right for their specific needs and abilities.

As a Conservative opposed to government spending, she might have been expected to be against increasing the education budget. In fact, she fought hard to get more money for Great Britain's educational system. She favored building more nursery schools and rebuilding older schools.

Edward Heath, the Conservative prime minister who gave Margaret Thatcher her first big break in politics in 1970 when he appointed her secretary of state for education.

Heath was a self-made and independent man. Highly educated, he had many interests outside politics. He was a skilled sailor (shown here aboard his own yacht, *Morning Cloud*), a scholar of economics and philosophy, and an expert organist and orchestra conductor.

Her record as education minister put her clearly on the side of improved educational opportunities. But in the public mind, she had a different claim to fame. As a money-saving measure, the Heath government quickly passed a bill denying free milk to older schoolchildren. The action aroused a storm of controversy. The amount of money saved was not great, and critics said that depriving children of milk was a terrible way to economize. As a result, the education minister became known as "Margaret Thatcher, the milk snatcher."

But the Heath government refused to back down on the milk issue. Edward (Ted) Heath had campaigned in 1970 on a program that was right in line with Margaret Thatcher's beliefs.

Like Thatcher, Heath came from a middle-class family, in contrast to many other Conservative leaders who had an upper-class background and inherited wealth. Like Margaret Thatcher, Heath believed in the classic Conservative philosophy that a free, competitive economy made businesses more efficient and led to economic growth and greater prosperity for all. Government planning, on the other hand, meant government handouts to save businesses that were inefficient.

This Conservative philosophy applied to individuals as well. People ought to help themselves instead

British miners picket a power station in February 1974. In support of their pay demands miners picketed oil-fired as well as coal-fired power stations, causing power shortages which plagued householders and disrupted industrial production.

A VC10 airliner of the British Overseas Aircraft Corporation (later called British Airways). For many years a government-run company, British Airways consistently lost money until the Thatcher government appointed new managers early in the 1980s. The unexpected turnaround confounded many of Mrs. Thatcher's critics.

of expecting the government to shower money on them. Benefits should only go to the truly needy, to the sick and the unemployed. In addition, taxes should be lowered. This would encourage and reward those who became successful through energy and initiative. It was these successful people who made the economy grow.

Since the end of World War II, the Conservative Party had been supporting Labor proposals for enlarging the welfare state and increasing governmental control of the economy. Conservatives had even gone along with Labor's program to nationalize industries such as the telephone and telegraph services, coal mining, steel, aviation, electricity, and transport. In Heath's opinion this was a mistake. The Conservative Party had to return to its true beliefs. It had to stop practicing what was called "consensus politics." Instead of echoing Labor ideas and enlarging the welfare state, it had to stand for its own principles of a free economy.

Heath's slogan was "Stand on your own feet." It applied to business, to workers, and to the Conservative Party as well.

In power, the Heath government set out to apply the classic Conservative philosophy to the British economy. It cut government spending, cut welfare and other benefits, lowered taxes, particularly for the rich, and passed the Industrial Relations Act, a law that greatly reduced the power of the unions. Heath hoped that all of these measures would stimulate economic growth.

March 3, 1974: The man with more votes but fewer seats. Heath leaves 10 Downing Street to drive to Buckingham Palace to hand in his resignation.

But the unions refused to obey the Industrial Relations Act. At the same time, unemployment began to rise. By July 1971 it was close to 3.5%, or 800,000 jobless, and increasing rapidly. The government then began to make more money available in the economy. It hoped this would help the economy to grow faster. Instead, inflation continued, and coal miners and other workers in Britain's nationalized industries struck for wage increases to keep pace with the rising cost of living.

Faced with growing inflation and unemployment, Ted Heath in 1972 made what has been called his U-turn. He went back to more government control over the economy and more government spending to help failing businesses.

One of the controls limited the wage increases that unions could receive. But this law did not reduce inflation. And the economy did not grow. Matters were made much worse by the oil crisis of 1973. In October 1973 the oil-producing countries of the Mideast cut oil supplies to Western nations. Then they raised the price of oil. By January 1974 oil cost four times more than it had in October 1973.

Higher oil prices raised inflation even further and made it more expensive for British companies to do business. This slowed the growth of the British economy.

The final blow to the Heath government came in the form of a second coal miners' strike. Beginning in November 1973, the miners and other unions sympathetic to them began a work slowdown to protest the wages offered by the Heath government.

In December Heath announced that a three-day work week would begin on January 1, 1974, to save fuel and power. Efforts to reach an agreement between the government and the miners were unsuccessful. On February 5 the miners voted to go out on strike two weeks later.

On February 7 Ted Heath called for an election to take place on February 28. He said that he needed the electorate's approval to deal with the oil crisis. But most Conservatives campaigned on the issue of the government's need to curb the unions.

The Conservatives got 300,000 more votes than Labor, which was led by former Prime Minister Harold Wilson. But in Great Britain the winning party is the one that wins the most seats in the House of Commons, not the one with the most votes. House candidates run in local districts all over the country. These local elections determine the outcome of the national election. In the February 28 election the Labor Party defeated the Conservatives in more local elections, thus winning more seats in the House. As a result, the Labor Party would form the new government.

Once more, Margaret Thatcher would be a member of the opposition. For four years she had dedicated herself mainly to educational matters. As a loyal but not powerful member of the Heath cabinet, she had watched from the sidelines as Heath and the leading players on his team put Conservative economic and financial policies into place. But they did not have enough faith in a free economy. Instead, they went back to government control and government spending. The result, she believed, was disaster for the economy and defeat in the election.

Margaret Thatcher still had faith in a free economy. She still believed in the Conservative philosophy. The problem seemed to be not in the policies but in the party leadership. And she had some ideas for changing that.

The crisis of 1973-74, when Arab oil producers raised their prices, made the contents of supertankers such as the one pictured here four times more expensive than they had been a year earlier. The price hike caused severe economic difficulties in many leading industrial nations, including Britain.

3

"No Room for Sympathy"

Harold Wilson and the Labor Party had won the February 1974 election by a very narrow margin. Labor only had five more seats than the Conservatives in the House of Commons. If Labor expected to govern for a full five-year term, it needed a larger majority.

The Labor government followed an obvious strategy. First it settled the miner's strike, which had almost shut down the economy. A week after the election the miners went back to work after accepting a wage increase of 22% to 32%. This was more than double what the Heath government had offered.

In Great Britain the party in power can hold a new election at any time. Prime Minister Wilson called for an election to take place in October 1974. He believed that his party was in a stronger position after settling the strike and would be able to increase its majority.

He was right. Labor again defeated the Conservatives, this time by a majority of 43 seats. Heath had now lost two elections in less than a year, and many Conservatives felt it was time for a change in the party leadership. Some younger members resented what they regarded as Heath's dictatorial

Veteran Labor Party leader Harold Wilson at a press conference in 1974. Wilson led the Labor Party to victory in two elections that year, taking advantage of the lack of leadership within the ranks of the Conservative Party.

Mrs. Thatcher, on the campaign trail, meets with supporters in Birmingham, one of Britain's major industrial centers.

Former Conservative Prime Minister Sir Alec Douglas-Home, who in 1974 devised new rules for the election of Conservative Party leaders. Under the new voting system Edward Heath lost his bid to retain the leadership in the 1975 Conservative Party elections.

ways. Most right-wing members of the party blamed him for going back on true Conservative principles when he made his U-turn. Among the rank-and-file, the back benchers, many felt that he had not governed well, had lost favor with the electorate, and ought to be replaced by a leader with greater popular appeal.

Heath tried to ignore the rising tide against him. Finally he agreed that an election for party leader should be held. The Labor Party had always elected its leader. But before 1965 the Conservative leader was chosen by a small group of the party's elder statesmen, the so-called "magic circle." Ted Heath had been the first leader chosen by a vote of the members, but no limit had been set on his term of office.

In December 1974 a committee headed by Sir Alec Douglas-Home presented new rules for electing the party leader. These rules called for elections once a year, with three ballots. The winner (referred to as "he" in the report) had to get a majority of the votes and lead his closest rival by at least 15%. These rules made it easier to defeat the leader in power. Many members of parliament called them "Alec's Revenge." Heath had replaced Douglas-Home as party leader in 1965.

The election was scheduled for February 1975. The leading candidate seemed to be Sir Keith Joseph, a right-wing intellectual who had been minister of state for social services in the Heath government. After the Conservative defeat in February 1974 Joseph began to speak out frequently about Ted Heath's failure to uphold basic Conservative Party principles. He had not reduced government spending, and he had not freed the economy from too much government control. What Joseph really objected to was that Heath had not cut down union power and had continued government spending in support of inefficient nationalized industries. Joseph's approach appealed to many in the party. But then Joseph made a serious mistake. In a speech in October 1974 he said that it might be a good idea to have forced birth control for people of "low intelligence." This was widely criticized as a racist statement directed at Britain's immigrant population. Joseph then withdrew from the election.

Enter Margaret Thatcher, who came forward as Joseph's replacement. They were friends and had similar philosophies. Joseph had schooled Thatcher in his right-wing economic theories. She would represent the same right-wing section of the party as Joseph. Thatcher said later of her decision to run, "I heard that Keith Joseph was not going to run against Ted. Someone had to. I said to Keith, 'If you are not, I shall.' There was no hesitation, there was no doubt, there has been no doubt since. It might have put me on the back benches for life, or out. I did not know. But the one thing I seemed to have was the power to make a decision when a decision had to be made."

When she announced her candidacy, Britain's bookmakers quoted odds of 50 to 1 against her victory. The first ballot was held on February 4. Ted Heath received 119 votes. Hugh Fraser, a back bencher, received 16. Margaret Thatcher received 130.

Heath immediately resigned, recognizing that he had been handed a humiliating defeat. Margaret Thatcher sent him off with some cool, hard words. "I will always be fond of dear Ted," she said, "but there is no room for sympathy in politics."

For the second ballot, three new candidates stepped forward. Among these, the most prominent was William Whitelaw, the former party chairman and a member of Heath's cabinet. The bookmakers quoted him as the heavy favorite. But, as Margaret Thatcher was happy to point out, the bookmakers had been wrong before.

The second ballot took place one week later. Over the weekend, Thatcher reminded the party of just where she stood. Speaking at the annual Young Conservative Conference, she said, "We want a mixed economy. But what else do we want? I believe we should judge people on their merits, not on their background; I believe a person who is prepared to work hard should receive greater rewards and keep them after taxes. I believe we should back workers not shirkers."

Sir Keith Joseph, initial favorite in the 1975 Conservative Party election for a new leader. Sir Keith, a right-wing intellectual, is a close friend of Mrs. Thatcher and shares many of her political views.

Mrs. Thatcher at home a few days before the first round of voting in the Conservative Party leadership election in February 1975.

Congratulatory kiss from husband Denis for Mrs. Thatcher on the occasion of her victory in the first round of voting in the Conservative Party leadership elections in 1975.

On the second ballot, Thatcher won a sweeping victory, beating Whitelaw by 146 votes to 79.

The word spread quickly through the House of Commons. "Maggie's done it." At the age of 49, Margaret Thatcher became the first woman to lead one of Britain's major political parties in the 700 years of parliamentary history. Maintaining her control even at this triumphant moment, Thatcher responded to a request to make a victory statement by walking up to the microphone and saying, "One . . . four . . . six . . . 146."

Actually, Thatcher's victory was less surprising than it seemed on the surface. First, she represented the anger and sense of failed hopes that many Conservatives felt after the party's dismal record in power from 1970 to 1974.

Second, not only in Great Britain but in many countries of the West, there was a growing right-wing sentiment. Its major theme was that too much government control was a danger to individual lib-

February 12, 1975: Mrs. Thatcher is triumphant! Elected first woman leader of the Conservative Party.

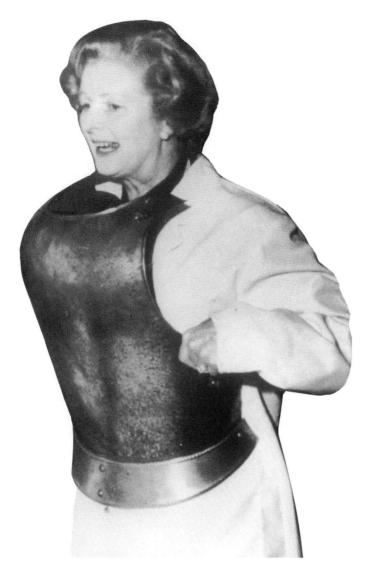

erty and to economic growth. Margaret Thatcher represented that belief as well.

And third, the House of Commons is a political arena in which a party leader's aggressive fighting style has always been very important. House members value a leader who has the ability to outmaneuver and outscore the opposition in questioning and debate. The Conservatives believed that Margaret Thatcher could be just this kind of a champion for them.

Mrs. Thatcher was a keen supporter of British membership in the European Economic Community. Here she is wearing a specially made sweater displaying the national flags of the nine member countries.

Mr. and Mrs. Thatcher decorating their recently acquired second home in 1975.

Their judgment was confirmed during the five years that Labor remained in power, from 1974 to the election of 1979. Thatcher was tough and unbending in her attacks on Labor and its policies. "She is a brilliant leader of the opposition," said William Whitelaw, the man she defeated for that role. "The best we have had for a long, long time."

Outside of parliament, Margaret Thatcher spoke out against the dangers of big government and of communism. She became, as British commentator Anthony Sampson has noted, "an international heroine of the right." So strongly did she attack the Soviet Union that its propagandists labeled her "The Iron Lady." It was a title that stuck—and one that Margaret Thatcher took pains to live up to.

From 1974 to 1979, the Labor government faced the problems of controlling inflation while trying to revive the declining British economy. (In 1975 inflation hit 27%; 1.5 million workers were unemployed; industrial production was falling.)

A major goal of Labor policy was to establish an agreement with the unions that would keep wage increases low in order to reduce inflation. Prime Minister Harold Wilson offered the unions what was called a "social contract." The unions would have to agree to hold down their wage demands. In exchange the government would follow policies that the unions wanted. Labor would try to create more jobs by increasing government spending to strengthen ailing businesses and industries. And it would tax wealth and high incomes while reducing the working man's tax burden.

In August 1975 the unions agreed to this proposal. Inflation had fallen to 14% by March 1976, when Wilson suddenly resigned, to the surprise of everyone in Britain except himself. He was replaced by James ("Sunny Jim") Callaghan, a veteran Labor Party leader who had been foreign secretary in Wilson's cabinet (the counterpart to America's secretary of state).

Callaghan also succeeded in getting the unions to agree to hold down their wage demands. From 1976 until the winter of 1978–79, Britain's unions generally went along with the policy of low wage

James ("Sunny Jim") Callaghan, the veteran politician who succeeded Harold Wilson as Labor prime minister in March 1976. Callaghan was the only party leader in modern British history without a university education. He had entered politics via the unions, and proved adept at handling them until the critical strikes staged by public service employees in the winter of 1978–79.

settlements. This helped to bring inflation down to 9%. It began to seem as if Labor was the only party that could control Britain's unions.

But Margaret Thatcher had never stopped attacking the Labor government for its failure to limit union power. In the winter of 1978–79—"the winter of discontent," as it came to be called—her criticism gained new force. The Labor Party suddenly faced a crisis brought on by a wave of strikes for higher wages by public service workers.

The strikes directly affected the everyday lives of millions of people. Sanitation workers, ambulance drivers, hospital employees, schoolteachers, even gravediggers stopped working. Garbage piled up on the streets, schools and hospitals all over the country shut down, the dead remained unburied.

The government was forced to give in to the union's demands for wage increases of up to 20%, far higher than Prime Minister Callaghan's ceiling of 5%.

Margaret Thatcher described the situation during the strikes as a return to "barbarism." "Our society," she said, "was sick—morally, socially, and economically. Children were locked out of school; patients were prevented from having hospital treatment; the old were left unattended in their wheelchairs."

She then predicted that the Labor Party was on its way out. "Whether or not they manage a few more abject months or weeks or even hours in office . . . Labor has passed the point of no return."

Thatcher was right. A month later, she put a motion before the House of Commons: "That this House has no confidence in Her Majesty's government." In the British system, the opposition party can make such a motion at any time. If the motion passes, the government has to call a new election. Since the governing party always has the most votes in the House, a motion of no confidence rarely wins.

In a dramatic and suspenseful scene, Thatcher's motion passed by one vote, 311 to 310. The government had fallen. An election would be held to choose a new government.

Mrs. Thatcher at the conclusion of a Conservative Party conference in 1976 predicts the issues over which the election of 1979 would eventually be fought. She appealed to "men and women of good will who do not want a Marxist future."

James Callaghan meets with striking members of the National Union of Public Employees in 1979.

Mrs. Thatcher's belief in a strong military was just as tough as her economic views. Here she drives a tank while visiting an armored regiment of the British Army of the Rhine in West Germany.

Mrs. Thatcher in April
1979 with leading mem-
bers of the Conservative
opposition a few weeks before the general election.

When the vote was announced, the Conservative
members of the House sent up a resounding cheer.
Margaret Thatcher smiled but remained silent. Later
she said, "A night like this comes once in a lifetime."

The next day, Prime Minister Callaghan saw the
Queen and asked her to dissolve parliament so
that new elections could be held. The campaign
would begin on April 7. Election Day was May 3.
"My troops are ready," Thatcher said. "They have
been ready for quite some time."

So was Thatcher. As she had said in 1975 after
she became the Conservative Party leader, "I've got
fantastic stamina and great physical strength, and
I have a woman's ability to stick to a job and get on
with it when everyone else walks off and leaves it.
I've got a lot to offer."

4

Making It

In 1979, for the first time in five years, the British people would choose a new government, and Margaret Thatcher had every reason to believe that it would be a Conservative government. As the election got under way, public opinion polls showed the Conservatives leading by ten percentage points and more. The feeling that the British people wanted a change, a new direction, was in the air.

For Britain, the seventies had been a rough and stormy decade. All of the leading industrial countries of the West, and Japan as well, had suffered economic difficulties as a result of the 1973 oil crisis and the resulting rise in oil prices. But Britain had been hit hardest. The levels of inflation and unemployment were higher in Britain than in any other European country. Its rate of economic growth was lower. For the first time since World War II, British working men and women experienced a drop in the level of their real income—the amount of food and other goods they could buy with their salary checks.

There were a few bright spots. By 1979 inflation had come down to 9%. And Britain was on her way to solving her energy crisis. By the end of 1977 the

Mrs. Thatcher enlists the help of the local livestock in her pitch for the rural vote in the campaign of 1979.

Mrs. Thatcher speaks at a Conservative local government conference in 1979. The "Labor Isn't Working" poster highlights the importance of the employment issue in the 1979 election. Unfortunately, unemployment continued to rise under the Conservatives.

Labor Prime Minister James Callaghan speaks in Portsmouth, England, during the 1979 election campaign.

new British oil fields in the North Sea were supplying half of the country's oil needs. By 1981 Britain would have a surplus of oil to sell to other countries.

But there remained a strong feeling in the country that all was far from well. The economy was not growing. Unemployment was high—1.3 million workers had no jobs. And there was a sense that British governments were unable to solve the most serious economic problems. Some people wondered if Britain was in a permanent decline. They even wondered if that decline might lead to revolution or the coming of communism.

In June 1975 the American journalist and broadcaster Eric Sevareid told an American television audience, "Britain is drifting slowly toward a condition of ungovernability." A short while later, Morley Safer, reporting for *60 Minutes*, declared that Britain had gone through "two decades of decline or crisis."

In 1977 a group of well-known English and American journalists and scholars contributed articles to a book about Great Britain called *The Future That Doesn't Work*. They concluded that Britain was in

Mrs. Thatcher takes part in a televised discussion concerning something she knew much about—the rise of women to top positions in business, education, government, and the media.

bad shape. It was "the sick man of Europe," and its economy and political structure were near collapse.

Margaret Thatcher was one of those who made plain her worries about the fate of her country. On a BBC (British Broadcasting Company) program, she said that continued Labor government would take Britain down the road to communism. "Each time you go further down the socialist road," she told her interviewer, "nearer and nearer to the communist state, then the consequences of the communist state will follow."

In Thatcher's opinion, the Labor government in power from 1974 to 1979 had clearly steered Britain towards socialism. It followed that communism was not far off. That was all the more reason to make sure the Conservatives won the 1979 election.

To a growing number of Britons, the most serious problem the country faced was the power of the unions. Before the 1979 election, public opinion polls showed that 89% of the population was

Mrs. Thatcher confers with former Conservative Prime Minister Harold Macmillan in February 1979. Macmillan was an old-fashioned conservative whose values were those of the Victorian era. Thatcher's, opponents say, are much the same.

worried about "excessive union power." That figure obviously included some of Britain's 12 million union members.

The strikes that disrupted people's lives during the "winter of discontent" in 1978–79 were still fresh in many voters' minds. They felt a strong sense of anger and frustration that the unions could do as they pleased, even if what they did made life unbearable for the rest of the country's citizens.

In fact, unions in Great Britain did have great power. Great Britain was the only industrialized country in the West with no laws making plain exactly what unions could and could not do. As a result, unions had a free hand.

If a union signed a contract with a business, it could later break that contract and go unpunished. If a local unit of a union wanted to go on strike even though national union leaders told them not to, the local went on strike. These "wildcat" strikes accounted for 95% of all the strikes that took place. If union members went on strike against, say, a bakery, they would also go on strike against companies that did business with the bakery, such as flour suppliers, box-makers, and trucking companies. This "secondary picketing" greatly increased the power of unions to tie up the economy by turning one strike into a series of strikes.

Even Prime Minister Callaghan's Labor government in the winter of 1978–79 had asked the unions voluntarily to agree not to use secondary picketing as a weapon. But the unions refused.

Yet, though British unions had great power, British workers were not doing very well. Their average take-home pay was about $125 a week, less than half of the amount earned by workers in most northern European countries. In the five years before the election of 1979, the wages of workers in Great Britain barely kept up with the rise in the cost of living.

The Labor Party was closely identified with the unions. Traditionally, its support came largely from union members. And the central governing body of the labor unions, the Trades Union Congress, had

Mrs. Thatcher's image is that of the toughest man we've got.
—HAROLD WILSON
former Labor prime minister

April 1979: Mrs. Thatcher introduces the Conservative "General Election Manifesto," a pamphlet outlining the direction a Conservative government would take if elected.

a strong and often controlling role in shaping the Labor Party's programs and policies. There was little doubt in the public's mind that the Conservative Party was far more likely to cut down the unions' power than the Labor Party.

As the four-week election campaign began on April 7, Margaret Thatcher and the Conservative Party were ready to take advantage of the public's anti-union feeling. As Thatcher said, "What we've been saying for ten to fifteen years is steadily being proven right. More and more people feel that way."

The Conservatives did not propose an all-out war on the unions. They knew that could tear the country apart. But they did promise to take some specific steps that would control union power. They would ban secondary picketing. They would protect workers from being fired for refusing to join a

Tight police security surrounds James Callaghan, campaigning on April 18, 1979, in a small town north of London. Callaghan's confidence was boosted just before the election when polls showed he was catching up fast with Mrs. Thatcher.

union. And they would make unions conduct votes by a secret ballot before going out on strike. Voting in secret would protect workers who did not want to strike from pressure by leaders and workers who did want to strike.

The rest of the Conservative program was based on two principles: tax cuts and economic freedom. Thatcher went before the voters expressing her belief that there must be a radical break with the past. The welfare state, with its nationalized industries, heavy public spending, and too-powerful unions, was stifling Great Britain's economic growth.

The welfare state must be cut back and the economy set free, Thatcher insisted. Taxes must be lowered. The government must begin to return nationalized businesses to private control. Only then would Britain be able to achieve solid economic growth. Only then would citizens be free to exercise their self-reliance and initiative to improve their lives and economic well-being.

In contrast, James Callaghan and the Labor Party offered voters a traditional Labor program. The choice, he said, was between a society that cared about its citizens and one that turned its back on them, particularly if they were less fortunate. The Labor government, Callaghan said, had "directly created and protected" 1.2 million jobs. "There is not a single part of the United Kingdom that would not suffer" from the Conservative policy of cutting the government spending that made the jobs program possible. The Conservatives would, in fact, turn much of England, Scotland, Wales, and Northern Ireland into "deserts of unemployment."

Specifically, the Labor platform called for a new "wealth tax" on the rich, for reduced spending on defense, and for doing away with the House of Lords, the upper chamber of Parliament. Members of the House of Lords were "nobles" with titles (barons, dukes, earls, etc.) as opposed to the "commoners" in the House of Commons. The House of Lords had always been strongly "Tory," or Conservative, in political belief. It had no real powers of its own, but its approval was required for all bills that passed in the House of Commons. If the Lords did not like a bill, they could not veto it, but they could delay it for up to a year. They often used this power to stall legislation that Labor wanted passed.

Interestingly, each party presented itself in this election as the exact opposite of its usual image. Labor was usually regarded as the party of change. Yet in 1979 it was insisting that it would carry on the best traditions of post–World War II British political life by maintaining the welfare state estab-

Concorde, the new Anglo-French supersonic airliner, entered service with British Airways in the 1970s when the company was still government-run. The *Concorde* fleet lost money until Thatcher appointed former captains of private industry to run British Airways. One of their first moves was to make the plane available for charter flights, which resulted in real profits.

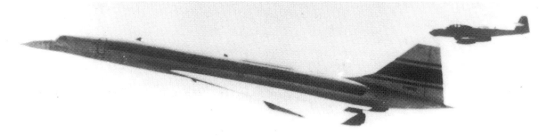

lished 25 years before. The Conservatives, usually viewed as the party of tradition and established custom, were insisting that what Britain needed was a radical break with the recent past.

As a candidate, Thatcher had some weaknesses. For one thing, she lacked experience in foreign affairs, as Labor Party politicians always pointed out. For another, her radical Conservatism might backfire. It was one thing to call for control and reform of the unions. In tradition-minded Britain, it could be quite another to insist on remaking society from scratch. There were also those in her own party who worried that her outspokenness might trip her up. She might make a comment that would reflect badly on her judgment or offend a particular group of voters.

Also, her style did not appeal to everyone. To some she seemed smug and self-righteous. She was so totally convinced of the power of her beliefs that she tended to address the voters like a parent lecturing a child. I really do know what's best, she seemed to say, so be good boys and girls and vote Conservative.

As the campaign moved toward election day, Margaret Thatcher hit hard on her main theme. "Change is coming," she said. "The slither and slide to the socialist state is going to be stopped, halted, and turned back."

James Callaghan, still trailing by ten points in the polls two weeks before election day, continued to maintain that he and the Labor Party would unite the country, while the Conservatives would divide it.

In the last week, there were signs that Labor was gaining ground. Callaghan and Thatcher had debated, and Callaghan seemed to have the better of it. His steady, low-key personality seemed to win out over Thatcher's sharper, slashing debating style. Polls showed Labor catching up fast, behind by just a couple of percentage points. Thatcher's campaign managers worried about her making a crucial mistake. But she made none. When the votes were counted, the desire for change was stronger than the appeal to tradition. Thatcher and the Con-

I do not like her. She is not like a man and not like a woman.
—VALERY GISCARD D'ESTAING
president of France

servatives won a solid victory. Their majority in the 635-member House of Commons was 43 seats.

Margaret Thatcher had become the first woman prime minister of Great Britain, and the first woman ever to head a major Western nation. In the traditional ceremony at Buckingham Palace, Queen Elizabeth officially designated her Great Britain's new prime minister and asked her to form a government.

Like the wives of countless previous prime ministers, Thatcher's husband, Denis, waited downstairs at the palace while his wife had her audience with the Queen.

The Thatchers then drove to 10 Downing Street, the official residence of the prime minister. Here, they hoped, they would spend the next five years—and more—cheered by a grateful nation celebrating its new days of glory.

5

The Iron Lady

To Margaret Thatcher political action was a personal thing. She had grown up listening to her father and the leading citizens of Grantham talk politics in the family grocery store, and she had been fascinated. Politics was a way to make things happen, to bring about change for the better. And politicians were the agents of this change.

Recalling this period, she said that by her late teens "politics was in my bloodstream."

Now she had reached the highest rung on Britain's political ladder. She was ready to translate her personal political ideals into a course of action for her country. As she saw it, her role was to rescue Great Britain from its 25-year slide toward socialism. She had a specific economic program to do this, a program that would change the direction and shape of the economy.

But equally important, perhaps more important, she wanted to bring about a change in the way Britons thought and acted. Specifically, what she had in mind was a return to the lost "Victorian values" of hard work, thrift, self-reliance, and a strong sense of duty. That, she believed, was precisely the great value of her economic policies. Once

Anthony Wedgwood Benn, a leading radical left-wing politician in post-war Britain, was one of the few politicians of any party to speak out against the use of military force to resolve the Falklands crisis.

October 1980: Mrs. Thatcher addresses the annual conference of the Conservative Party. She appealed to the nation, and especially the unions, calling for a "winter of common sense," a reference to the strikes of 1978–79, "the winter of discontent."

Mrs. Thatcher makes her first appearance as prime minister at the annual Conservative Party Conference in October 1979.

in effect, they would restore these values to their deserved place in British life.

The important thing, she felt, was not to compromise. She remembered Ted Heath's U-turn and the disastrous result it produced. She knew that British political life since World War II had been built on compromise. Conservatives had joined with Laborites in establishing and enlarging the welfare state. This was part of what was called "the consensus," an agreement by both parties that the state had a duty to maintain high employment and to use the power of the government to solve its citizens' problems.

Margaret Thatcher did not believe that the consensus had been good for Great Britain. She believed in a free economy. She believed that her conservative economic program was the way to turn back from the consensus, to save Britain from socialism and the welfare state.

As she often said proudly, "I am not a consensus politician. I am a conviction politician. . . . The reason I am in politics is because I believe in certain things and try to put them into practice."

And put them in practice she did, but not with the results she had hoped for. Twenty-one months later, in February 1981, Margaret Thatcher rose from the government front bench to respond to the jeers and insults of the opposition. Since her economic program had become law, Great Britain had slipped down a steep slope into the worst recession since the depression of the 1930s, when millions of Britons stood in line to get a bowl of soup at soup kitchens. Ten percent of the work force, close to 2.5 million people, were out of work. And there was no relief in sight. All signs indicated that unemployment would rise to 3 million before the end of 1981.

But Margaret Thatcher remained confident and unafraid. In calm, unemotional words, she coolly explained to parliament that until competition was

Anthony Wedgwood Benn (fourth from left), a former Labor minister, marches at the head of a demonstration protesting Conservative employment policies.

restored, until the government stopped spending money, the economy would not recover.

"Same old story," shouted a left-wing member of the Labor Party.

"Of course it's the same old story," Thatcher snapped back. "Truth usually is the same old story."

Margaret Thatcher's confidence cheered those who believed in her. But many in Britain had their doubts. Not only was the economy beset by high unemployment. Interest rates had soared to 22%. Inflation had roller-coastered up to 22% in the summer of 1980. In early 1981 it stood at 15%, 5% higher than when the Conservatives won election in May 1979. A record number of 10,000 businesses had gone bankrupt during the Thatcher government's first year in office. And the economy was operating close to 5% below its level during the last year of the Labor government.

Some of the strongest critics were in Margaret Thatcher's own Conservative Party, including former prime minister Ted Heath. But she insisted that she had set Britain on the right course. She had campaigned to cut government spending, to reduce income taxes, to do away with government support for businesses that could not prosper on their own. She had promised to restore competition, even if that meant allowing weak and inefficient businesses to die. Above all, she was determined to get inflation under control.

Her economic program was supposed to achieve all these goals. She cut income taxes from 80% to 60% for those earning more than $50,000 a year, and from 33% to 30% for those below $50,000. She raised the value-added tax, a sales tax on all but the most essential goods, to 15%. Theoretically, this would stop consumers from overspending and thus hold down inflation. Finally, she cut government spending on foreign aid, housing, and the services supplied by towns, villages, and cities all across the country.

Basically, Thatcher's economic policy was based on the ideas of a conservative American economist, Milton Friedman. Thatcher's chief economic adviser, Sir Keith Joseph, secretary of industry in her

Mrs. Thatcher's official portrait, taken in 1981 by the famous British photographer Norman Parkinson.

cabinet, believed firmly in Friedman's theories of monetarism. According to these theories, economic growth and inflation were both controlled by the amount of money the government put into the economy. In Britain's case, believers in monetarism insisted, it was too much government spending that had been the chief cause of inflation. If the government spent less, put less money into the economy, inflation could be controlled. In addition, governments that taxed their citizens at a high rate were always tempted to spend more because

> *This country will come through by getting efficient and having honest, sound money.*
> —MARGARET THATCHER

Mrs. Thatcher protects Britain's interests at a European Economic Summit meeting in Luxembourg in the spring of 1981.

they had the money from taxation to spend. Hence, tax rates should be lowered in order to lessen the government's temptation to spend.

But when this theory was put to the test in Great Britain through Thatcher's program, it did not work the way it was supposed to. High interest rates and the high sales taxes stopped businesses and individuals from spending. The economy went into a decline. Unemployment rose. Then the government had to spend more because it was obligated to pay workers their unemployment insurance.

At the same time, Britain was caught in a global

> *Any leader has to have a certain amount of steel in them, so I am not that put out about being called the Iron Lady.*
>
> —MARGARET THATCHER

OUR
E BLUE
ENTINE

AGGIE

February 1981: Delegates
to the National Conference
of the Young Conservatives
demonstrate their affec-
tion for Mrs. Thatcher, who
was always especially popular with the younger
members of her party.

69

Mrs. Thatcher and senior Conservative ministers at the State Opening of Parliament in April 1981.

recession. Economic activity went into a slump throughout the world, and British industry had trouble selling its goods and services. In Great Britain, nationalized industries owned by the government (such as British Steel, British Leyland, a car maker, and British Airways), all saw a strong decline in their profits. The Thatcher government had to choose between allowing these industries to go bankrupt or giving them assistance so they could stay in business.

It was against the Thatcher philosophy to give them money. But if they did not get the money they needed, they would shut down. Hundreds of thousands of workers would join the ranks of the unemployed, and the government would have to pay for their unemployment benefits. Faced with this reality, the Thatcher government did the only thing it could do. It gave the companies the money they needed.

In the end, instead of decreasing, government

spending during Thatcher's first 21 months in office went up sharply. It was for this reason that Milton Friedman insisted his theories had not had a fair test. He also pointed out that the Thatcher government had given government employees a 28% raise and had taken other steps that added to inflation.

Pressure began to mount in the country for Margaret Thatcher to change her economic policies. It came from Conservative Party members as well as from the opposition Labor Party. In September 1980, at the annual Conservative Party Conference, Thatcher faced a revolt from middle-of-the-road Conservatives who had not been enthusiastic about her economic policies from the start. Thatcher called these unenthusiastic members "wets," British slang for those who are prone to waver from their principles.

In a dramatic speech to the conference, she declared that she would not change her policies. She would see them through because she was convinced she was right. There would be no repeat of Ted Heath's disastrous U-turn of 1972. "This lady's not for turning," she insisted to the cheers of her right-wing supporters in the party. (The phrase was a reference to a famous play by the English dramatist Christopher Fry, *The Lady's Not for Burning.*)

Still, in February 1981, six months after she had triumphed over her critics at the party conference, Margaret Thatcher could point to no improvement in the economic situation. In fact, things had become worse, and there were renewed calls for a change in course. Many Britons were pessimistic about the future of the country and doubtful that

American economist Dr. Milton Friedman of the University of Chicago, whose "monetarist" theories influenced Mrs. Thatcher's economic policies. Her opponents regarded Friedman's doctrines of "tight credit" and reduced government spending as essentially academic and dangerous in the context of dealing with a struggling economy.

Thatcher had the right answers. Public opinion polls showed that the Conservative Party was 13% behind the Labor Party in public favor. And only 31% of all Britons approved of Thatcher's leadership.

Yet, even with high unemployment and the continued decline in the economy, the reaction of Britain's citizens was generally peaceful. There were demonstrations by the unemployed, but there were no angry mobs marching on Parliament. The people remained somewhat protected by benefits of the welfare state. Workers who were fired or laid off received severance pay (a cash payment based on the number of years they had worked for the company) and regular unemployment benefits. Those with children also got income tax refunds and rent reductions if the family lived in public housing. Children received free milk and free lunches at school.

But there were those who warned that bitterness and anger would increase if economic hard times continued too much longer. There might be violence and perhaps even a movement against democratic government.

When she took office, Margaret Thatcher had said it would take at least 18 months for her policies to begin to change things. But six months after she became prime minister, the economy was already in a steep downturn. It was then that she spoke of "the first five years and the five years after that."

Fifteen months later, in February 1981, most Britons did not want to give Thatcher even her first five years. The consensus was that she had about a year to turn the economy around. If she failed, her own party would undoubtedly move against her. As one Conservative senior minister pointed out, the party itself would force a change: "If, after another year to 15 months, there are no signs of an upturn in the economy and a reduction in unemployment, I would expect a cabinet consensus to force a change of policy. If Thatcher agreed, there need not be any change, except in policy. If she disagreed, it would go to a vote in the cabinet, and if she were defeated, she would have to go."

If you have a sense of purpose and a sense of direction, I believe people will follow you. Democracy isn't just about deducing what the people want. Democracy is leading the people as well. —MARGARET THATCHER

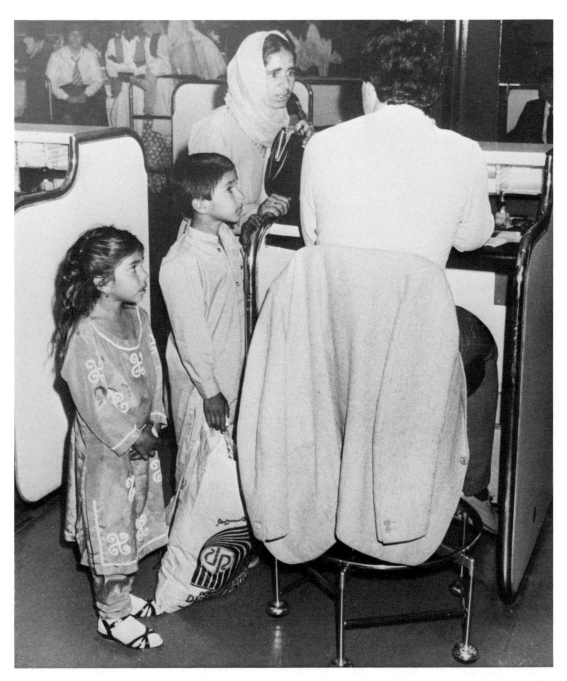

A Pakistani woman and her two children speak to an immigration officer at London's Heathrow Airport. Hundreds of thousands of emigrants from Pakistan, India, the British West Indies, and other former British colonies arrived in London after the 1950s. Amid high unemployment and racial tension, Thatcher sharply restricted immigration quotas in 1986.

6

"I Quite Like Being Prime Minister"

In the spring of 1981, Britons reacted with fear and dismay as their economy continued to decline, as more and more businesses went "bottoms up," as unemployment lines grew longer and longer.

Those who thought Margaret Thatcher's policies were right mostly kept silent and crossed their fingers.

Those who disapproved were outspoken in their anger. They accused her of not caring about the pain and suffering of the unemployed. Union leaders and union members bombarded her with a barrage of criticism. The *New Statesman,* a traditionally anti-Conservative magazine, had long ago dubbed her "Attila the Hen." Every week, for the past 12 months, Britain's most prestigious newspaper, the *Sunday Times,* had been publishing a "body count" of the newly unemployed, titled "Jobless Britain."

Friend and foe alike could only watch in fascination, however, as Margaret Thatcher dominated the life of the country and occupied the center of the political arena as no prime minister had done since the wartime days of Winston Churchill. To some, her prime ministership seemed like a long-running

"Attila The Hen"? This strictly unofficial portrait of Mrs. Thatcher was part of a London exhibition by German artist Hans Haacke in 1984. The pose, reminiscent of official portraits of Britain's Queen Victoria (*d.* 1901), amused Mrs. Thatcher's opponents, who consider her values those of the Victorian era.

A member of the black community confronts a London policeman during the Brixton riots in April 1981. The disturbances in London and other British cities revealed divisions in British society for which Mrs. Thatcher's immediate prescription was an increase in police powers.

10 Downing Street, official London residence of British prime ministers. At least one policeman is on duty outside at all times. The police presence is increased whenever British security chiefs suspect the possibility of terrorism against top officials.

TV drama, a show whose script specialized in bad news and whose leading lady was a bossy and talkative scene stealer. She produced the show and gave herself the best lines. She delighted in putting down the other actors, and sometimes the audience as well. She insisted that no matter what the ratings said, whether the audience liked it or not, the show was exactly what they needed to stiffen their backbones and firm up their souls. And beyond that, she was having a terrific time.

Some of her fellow Conservatives complained publicly (but anonymously) about her personality—her bossiness, her tendency to put people down, her annoyance at being criticized, her dislike of having to hear the other side of any given question. "When she gets into an argument," said one, "she talks all the time. Talk. Talk. Talk." Another declared: "She can be very sharp, steely in cutting somebody short if she has lost interest in what is being said."

But no one could say that she didn't devote herself to her job. Living in the apartment above her office at 10 Downing Street, she was, as a number

April 1981: A police van overturned by black youths blazes in Brixton. Mrs. Thatcher came down firmly on the side of law and order, refusing at first to be influenced by the wider implications of the riots, such as unemployment and poor relations between the police and the black population.

The Brixton riots caused extensive damage to property in the area. Police and fire services were severely tested by these unexpected disturbances.

of commentators pointed out, repeating her experience of living above the grocery store in Grantham. She impressed her staff with her "terrific appetite for work and her energy level." She got by on five hours of sleep a night, was up at 6:30 A.M., made breakfast for herself and Denis, and was in her office by 9:00 A.M.

Until bedtime, she worked steadily. If she had no official lunch to attend, she ate at her desk. She usually had dinner at the House of Commons with Conservative M.P.s (members of parliament). If she entertained in the evening, the conversation almost always revolved around political matters. If she did not entertain, she did her paperwork.

"There's no magic formula," she confessed when asked how she managed to keep up her pace. "The only secret is that I love this job. It suits me and stimulates me. There's never been one moment when I thought, 'Oh, my goodness, I wish I wasn't here.' "

London policemen, crouched behind their protective shields, attempt to clear rioting youths from the streets of Brixton in 1981.

Twice a week, on Tuesday and Thursday afternoons, she went to the House of Commons for "question days," the traditional ritual in which the prime minister responds to questions from members. At these sessions, and whenever she was in the House presenting, explaining, or defending her policies, she was charged-up and ready for battle. She loved it, and she admitted as much. "The adrenalin flows," she said. "They really come out fighting at me, and I fight back. I stand there and I know, 'Now come on, Maggie, you are wholly on your own. No one can help you.' And I love it."

In what might be described as the only nonpolitical acts in her routine, she had her hair done twice a week by a hairdresser who came to 10 Downing Street. In fact, soon after she took office, she changed her hair color to a darker shade of blond—at the advice of her political consultant. As part of her political image, she never appeared in public unless she was perfectly dressed and groomed, with every hair in place. This seemed to reflect her natural inclination to maintain order and control.

It was exactly the order and control she valued so much that broke down in April 1981. Those who had feared violence as economic hardship mounted saw their fears come true. It began in a dirt-poor district of south London called Brixton, whose population was 36% black. Rebelling against what they saw as police brutality, young blacks took out their frustration, resentment, and anger on their surroundings. Using bricks, stones, iron bars, petrol bombs, and whatever other homemade weapons came to hand, they went on a rampage. The rioting spread to 30 towns and cities in Great Britain, including Liverpool, Manchester, and 20 neighborhoods in London. The riots lasted for 10 days and caused millions of dollars' worth of damage. More than 1,500 policemen were injured, and 3,000 people were arrested.

The riots sent a shock wave through British society. How and why had such violence erupted in a country so proud of its tradition of peaceful and civil behavior? Margaret Thatcher declared that the days of the riots were her worst days as prime

The lack of communication between the police and the black community determined the ferocity of the confrontation, especially in Brixton, where relations had been tense for several years. Mrs. Thatcher later ordered an investigation of police behavior before and during the riots.

minister. The situation seemed desperate.

Many people thought that the high unemployment rate among British youth—34% as compared to 11% overall—was one of the main causes of the riots. It was unemployment, not racial prejudice or police brutality, that was the problem, they said. Job training programs were the solution.

But Margaret Thatcher didn't see it that way. She toured the riot area in Liverpool and saw the destruction. More than a mile of the city had been devastated. Riding in her black bullet-proof Jaguar, she was pelted with tomatoes and rolls of toilet paper.

Thatcher refused to go along with those who called for job programs, including some members of her own cabinet. The solution, she insisted, was not government spending on job training but tougher police action. In the House of Commons, she said that she would not even begin to think

Riots erupted later in 1981 in other British cities. Police in Liverpool (pictured here) had to contend with rioting which was not confined simply to the black population. Popular discontent with government policy was becoming more widespread.

Unemployment remained a critical issue throughout 1981. Here, in June, Michael Foot, Callaghan's successor as leader of the Labor Party, visits a demonstration by the jobless.

about economic measures until law and order was restored. The government, she announced, would propose a new law giving the police more power against rioters, including the right to use tear gas, water cannons, and plastic bullets. (In Liverpool during the riots, the police had received special permission to use tear gas against crowds for the first time in British history.)

But the matter did not end there. There was a growing number of Conservatives who opposed "Thatcherism," as Thatcher's policies had come to be called. They insisted that the monetarist doctrine of cutting public spending and holding down the money supply was bringing the country to ruin.

In August, Thatcher was forced to retreat from her hard-line stand on job training. This meant compromising on a key point of Thatcherism, spending government money. At a cabinet meeting, moderate ministers led by Employment Secretary James Prior insisted that the government do something about unemployment among the young. Thatcher was reluctantly forced to agree to a $1.3 billion job training and education program for Great Britain's 900,000 unemployed young people. "Margaret came under very heavy fire," said one moderate cabinet minister after the meeting.

Even before this defeat, Thatcher had decided to do something about her "wet," and as she saw it, disloyal ministers. On September 14 she made her move, banishing the doubters from the cabinet. She fired Prior and a number of other moderates, replacing them with staunch right-wingers whose loyalty to her and her policies was unquestioned. It was a swift and daring move that reinforced her image of toughness, as well as her total commitment to her policies.

This action set the stage for the annual Conservative Party Conference in October. Unemployment had gone up a notch to 12%. Thatcher's approval rating stood at 28%. The *Times* of London said that her government had "lost popular support." Many Conservatives felt the same way. They were worried about the growing popularity of the new Social Democratic Party, which had allied itself with the Liberal Party as a center group to stand against the policies of both Labor and the Conservatives. Public opinion polls showed strong support for the Social Democrats, and many Conservatives saw the new party as a threat to their reelection.

At the Conservative Party Conference, a determined group of Conservative back benchers and senior party members launched an attack on Thatcher's policies and leadership. Speaking at the conference, former prime minister Ted Heath called for increased government spending to halt the economic decline. The high unemployment rate, he

James Prior was secretary of state for employment at the time of the Brixton riots in 1981. His insistence that the government face the problem of unemployment among the young alienated him from Mrs. Thatcher, who finally sacked Prior and other moderates from her cabinet on September 14, 1981.

said, was "morally unjustified." Furthermore, he reminded the delegates that failure to combat high unemployment had led to dictatorship in Germany and war in Europe in the 1930s.

But Thatcher still had overwhelming control of the party. The revolt got nowhere. In a closing speech to the conference, Thatcher slammed the door in the face of her opponents. "I will not change just to court popularity," she declared firmly. "There are those who say our nation no longer has the stomach for the fight. I think I know our people. They do."

For all her public display of confidence, Thatcher's fate depended on what happened to the economy, which was showing no signs of improvement.

In the meantime, however, Thatcher began to redeem her campaign promise to move against the labor unions. She was well aware that polls showed 30% of the public favoring a restriction of union rights. By responding to this strong anti-union feeling, she could both gain political advantage and satisfy her philosophical convictions. After her election in 1979, Thatcher held back from proposing laws that would curb the unions. For the first two and one-half years of her government, her chief strategy was to ignore the heads of the unions and appeal directly to the workers. In a number of instances, workers listened to Thatcher and their employers and disobeyed union orders to strike. The heart of her message to the workers was that if they did not accept proposed wage increases they might lose their jobs. She emphasized that in a time of high unemployment it might be difficult for them to find new jobs. Workers recognized the power of this argument as more and more of them were laid off and more and more businesses went bankrupt.

Union leaders said Thatcher's approach amounted to blackmail. They charged that she was deliberately doing nothing about unemployment in order to weaken or break the labor unions.

Now, in November 1981, the Thatcher government decided to go a step further and try to restrict union rights by law. This law would abolish

For this government, it is not the first 100 days that count. It is the first five years and the five years after that. We have to move this country in a new direction, to change the way we look at things, to create a wholly new attitude of mind.

—MARGARET THATCHER

the unions' right to strike for political reasons, in support of or in opposition to a government policy. It would also make it more difficult for unions to put pressure on workers who refused to join a union. And it would make it illegal for government agencies dominated by the Labor Party to require that government construction projects employ only union labor.

The unions were, of course, furious at this development. The general secretary of the 11-million-member central union organization, the Trades

Mrs. Thatcher visits a factory. While aware of unemployment problems, she maintained that her economic programs would eventually create employment once British business became more competitive.

Belgian police carry away an injured Italian soccer fan after rioting English fans killed 38 and injured 200 during the 1985 European Cup Final game in Brussels. The riot capped a decade of fan violence at British soccer matches and prompted the Thatcher government to enact stiff laws to curb "football hooliganism," which, studies showed, was partly caused by joblessness among frustrated working-class youths.

Union Congress, said the proposed law would mean "sweeping restrictions" on unions. The Thatcher government stood its ground and hinted that it would propose even stronger anti-union measures in the future.

As far as public opinion was concerned, Margaret Thatcher won that argument. In March 198 she made a second move designed to win popular approval. She had said at the Conservative Party Conference in October that she would not change to "court popularity." But in March, despite her long-standing opposition to government spending, she presented a new budget that contained $2.35 billion for expanding the economy. The public cheered, though Labor pointed out that there was no money in the budget to fight unemployment, now at 13% and still rising.

A few days after the budget was presented, a public opinion poll showed the Conservative Party leading Labor for the first time since 1979.

Thatcher and the Conservatives displayed great optimism. The worst days of economic decline were over, they insisted. Inflation had dropped from 12% to 11% and was forecast to decline below 1%. In addition there had been a recent cut in the price of North Sea oil. This would further stimulate the expansion of the economy, according to the Conservatives.

Most economists doubted that the worst of the recession in Great Britain was indeed over. Thatcher would have to face a new election in May 1984, when her term expired. The general opinion was that unless the economy improved dramatically—which was not considered likely—she would surely lose. And the prospect remained that despite her 43-vote majority, she might even lose a vote of confidence if the economy worsened.

And then, on April 2, 1982, Argentina invaded the Falkland Islands—and everything changed.

British politician Sir Ian Gilmour, a moderate member of the Conservative Party who lost his cabinet position in Thatcher's government when she fired a number of "wets" (as moderate Conservatives were known) in September of 1981. Sir Ian rarely disguised his opposition to Mrs. Thatcher's policies, even criticizing her in newspaper interviews.

TAL CUAL

Año 5 - N° 129 - 4-6-82
Editorial Perfil S.A.
Buenos Aires - Argentina
$ 15.000
En Uruguay N$ 17

Contó su tía Agatha:

- **Odia a la Reina Isabel**
- **Envidia a Lady Di porque es joven**
- **Quiso ser Miss Universo y fracasó**
- **Se operó la panza para adelgazar**

LA THATCHER ESTA LOCA. SE CREE LA MUJER MARAVILLA

7

The Falklands Factor

When it began, officials in Britain called it "a little local difficulty." About 2,500 Argentine troops, part of an invading force that included an aircraft carrier and three destroyers, came ashore on the two major Falkland Islands, East and West Falkland, in the hours before dawn on April 2. They engaged 40 Royal Marines in a gun battle at Port Stanley, the largest settlement on West Falkland. After three hours of fighting, the Marines surrendered. Argentina could claim that it had taken back the islands it long had called its own. The conquest included the Falklands, South Georgia, and the South Sandwich Islands. These three archipelagos, or scattered groups of islands, extended from 400 to 1,500 miles off the east coast of South America.

The first question many asked was, why all the fuss? The islands themselves were bare, rocky, treeless bumps in the Atlantic, of little economic value. The media talked of a "comic opera" dispute. But for Argentina, the islands represented a matter of national pride. In addition, the military government that had taken over the country in 1976 was losing popular support as inflation skyrocketed to 143% a year and unemployment soared. The real

May 3, 1982: Francis Pym with UN Secretary General de Cuellar at a news conference in New York. Attempts to negotiate a settlement continued throughout the conflict.

At the time of the invasion, few Argentines thought Britain would attempt to retake the islands by force. Once Mrs. Thatcher decided on a military solution, they thought she was mad. This Argentine magazine headline reads "Thatcher is crazy. She thinks she is Wonder Woman."

reason for the Falklands invasion, some observers said, was to take people's minds off the dismal economy.

Eight thousand miles away, in Great Britain, Margaret Thatcher decided on a military response. She said her decision was based on principle. Argentina's invasion, she pointed out, was naked aggression, a violation of the code of behavior among civilized nations. For that reason it could not be tolerated. In diplomatic talks with Argentina, Great Britain had always said that it would abide by the wishes of the islanders. If they wanted to shift their allegiance from Britain to Argentina, the British

An Argentine soldier patrols a street in the Falklands. Argentine forces were generally considerate to the British population. Relations became less friendly when the fighting started in earnest.

government would allow Argentina to take over the islands peacefully. But the Falklanders had always remained loyal to Britain. Argentina, Thatcher insisted, could not take by force what it had been unable to achieve by diplomacy.

The lines were drawn. What had started as a "comic opera" war gathered steam and suddenly turned into a bloody battle in which modern, sophisticated weapons would take hundreds of lives, and which, for three months, would involve all the major nations of Europe and Latin America as cheering bystanders on one side or the other. It would also cause severe problems for American diplomacy and threaten relations between the United States and Russia, which flirted with providing active assistance to Argentina.

Great Britain's response came quickly. At an emergency session of the House of Commons, Labor and Conservative members voted almost unanimously for a motion directing the government to take back the islands by force if it could not do so through negotiations. The able and respected foreign secretary in the Thatcher government, Lord Carrington, resigned as a matter of honor because his department had failed to anticipate the Argentine invasion. He was replaced by Francis Pym, who was considered Thatcher's chief rival in the Conservative Party. Pym had criticized her earlier decision to reduce Britain's conventional navy forces. His appointment underlined Thatcher's weakened position at this point. She was also hurt by accusations from both Conservatives and Laborites that she had failed to take precautions against the invasion. But she was determined to regain her strength by forcing Argentina to back down.

Immediately Thatcher set in motion a strategy to use force if necessary. A 40-ship task force began to assemble off the coast of Great Britain. On board were some 2,000 troops, including Queen Elizabeth's middle son, Prince Andrew, a helicopter pilot on the aircraft carrier HMS *Invincible*. The force would steam down to the South Atlantic and establish a blockade of the islands. At this point, Great Britain insisted that its sole object was to drive the

Francis Pym became Britain's foreign secretary when Lord Carrington resigned. Carrington considered he had failed in his duty by not anticipating the Argentine invasion.

Argentine troops from the islands and restore British control.

At the same time, Great Britain froze Argentine assets of $1.5 billion in Britain. Argentina responded by freezing British assets worth $5.8 billion in Argentina. But Great Britain was clearly winning the battle of public opinion. The United Nations Security Council voted 10 to 1 in favor of a British resolution demanding that Argentina withdraw from the islands. Also, all Britain's partners in the European Economic Community (Common Market) voted to impose economic sanctions on Argentina. Only the United States refused to support the British position officially. The Reagan administration wanted to remain friendly with Argentina because it felt Argentina could help fight

The British task force continues the journey south. Exercises were held continuously throughout the voyage. Here, a Sea Harrier jump jet prepares to take off from the aircraft carrier HMS *Hermes.*

Argentines wait for news of the fighting, outside the offices of the national newspaper, *La Nación.*

communism in Central and South America. Instead of backing either side the United States sent Secretary of State Alexander Haig off on a round of shuttle diplomacy between Buenos Aires and London. But Haig's attempt to mediate an agreement between the two countries ended in failure.

As the task force set sail in the second week of April, Margaret Thatcher spoke of her determination to get the islands back. "We have to recover those islands," she said in a television interview.

"We must use all our professionalism, our flair, every single bit of native cunning and all our equipment. We must go out calmly, quietly, to succeed." British public opinion was solidly behind her. One poll showed that 83% of the British people wanted to reclaim the Falklands and 53% favored the use of force to achieve that goal.

Thatcher was sure that Argentina would not withdraw unless it was convinced that Britain would use force. In the House of Commons, Foreign Secretary Pym declared, "Britain does not appease dictators." And when Thatcher was greeted with renewed demands that she resign, she coolly replied, "No. Now is the time for strength and resolution."

In the end, Britain mounted a D-day landing operation and sent its men ashore in the teeth of fire from Argentine planes and Argentine defend-

An antiaircraft gunner on alert at Comodoro Rivadavia in southern Argentina, the main base of operations for Argentine air attacks on the British fleet. Argentine pilots faced the risk of running out of fuel on return flights, since the Falklands were at extreme range for their aircraft.

British troops come ashore in the Falklands, securing their foothold on the islands. The Scimitar light tank is dug into a defensive firing position. British forces suffered unexpectedly high casualties during the landings, and were not convinced that victory would come easily.

ers on the island. It took a British armada of 98 ships to achieve victory 10 weeks after the Argentine invasion. British Major General Jeremy Moore accepted the Argentine surrender and sent this message back to Margaret Thatcher in London: "The Falklands are once more under the government desired by their inhabitants. God save the Queen."

The costs of victory were not small. It was estimated that 1,000 Argentinian soldiers lost their lives in the war. There were 255 British dead and 777 wounded. Great Britain lost $1.4 billion in military equipment.

But for Margaret Thatcher, the Falklands War was clearly a triumph. Upon receiving word of the Argentine surrender, she declared, "Today has put the Great back in Britain." A cheering, happy crowd gathered in front of 10 Downing Street and sang "Rule, Britannia," an old anthem celebrating the invincibility of the British navy. Thatcher came out to join the crowd, shaking every hand within reach and saying, "This is a great vindication of everything we have done. It proves what we thought was right. What a night this has been for Britain! What a wonderful victory!"

In fact, the Falklands War changed the face of British politics—and the fate of Margaret Thatcher. Before the war, her popularity was at a low ebb. She was seen as a faltering leader whose economic policies were not working and who faced certain defeat in the next election, barring an economic miracle. After the war, her fortunes were suddenly reversed. The British people seemed to forget their

Mrs. Thatcher and her husband made a surprise visit to the Falklands (January 1983), where they toured Port Stanley airfield. The Falklands later became a major training ground for the British army.

economic woes as they gloried in Great Britain's rebirth as a powerful nation that could fight triumphantly for a just cause. "The Falklands factor," as the effect of the war came to be called, made all the difference.

For the rest of 1982 and on into the spring of 1983, there was little change in the decline of the British economy. Yet public opinion polls showed Thatcher's popularity holding strong. Thatcher and the Conservatives were favored by 49% of the Brit-

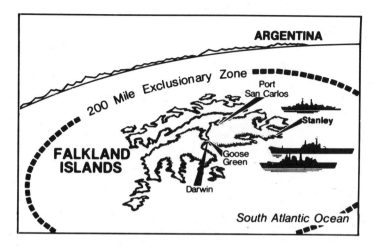

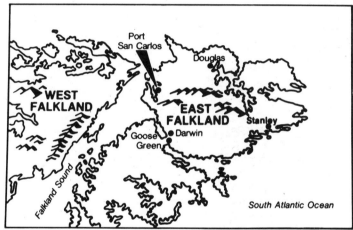

Chronicle of
THE FALKLAND WAR

March 19 Argentine transport lands metal workers on South Georgia—raise Argentine flag

April 2 Argentine forces invade Falklands—British Marines surrender in Stanley

April 3 South Georgia and South Sandwich Islands seized by Argentina

April 5 British armada sets sail for Falklands

April 12 Britain imposes 200-mile war zone

April 25 British forces invade South Georgia

April 26 South Georgia capture completed

May 1 Stanley airfield attacked by air and sea—Argentine planes attack fleet

May 2 Submarine sinks Argentine cruiser General Belgrano

May 4 Another air attack on Stanley and Goose Green —Argentine fighter sinks H M S Sheffield with missile

May 7 Britain extends total exclusion zone to within 12 miles of the Argentine coast

May 10 British warships bombards positions around Stanley —Argentine tanker sunk

May 12 Argentine planes attack British fleet

May 15 British commandoes raid Pebble Island airstrip —eleven Argentine aircraft destroyed

May 16 Argentine supply ships attacked in Falkland Sound—Stanley airfield bombed

May 21 Beachhead established at San Carlos port —frigate H M S Ardent sinks,five frigates damaged

May 22 5,000 British troops land

May 23 British frigate H M S Antelope sunk

May 25 British destroyer H M S Coventry sunk and container ship Atlantic Conveyor abandoned

May 28 Darwin and Goose Green captured

May 29 1,400 Argentine troops captured at Darwin and Goose Green—Argentine positions at Douglas and Teal Inlet taken

June 8 Argentine planes hit British landing ships Sir Galahad and Sir Tristan

June 11-12 British advance to within 10 miles of Stanley —400 prisoners taken

June 14 Surrounding hills of Stanley taken by British —Argentines in retreat—surrender talks begin

June 15 14,800 Argentine troops laid down their arms and surrender to British forces at Stanley

A chronicle of the key events in the war between Argentina and Great Britain.

ish public, as opposed to only 34% for Labor and 15% for the Social Democratic/Liberal Alliance. It made good sense for Margaret Thatcher to call an election at this point, a year before her five-year term would end. The one bright spot in the economic picture was inflation, which was down to 4% but was expected to begin rising again. Now was the time. Thatcher called for elections to be held on June 9.

The four-week election campaign did nothing to dim Thatcher's confidence that she would win easily. The Labor Party was totally disorganized by a continuing conflict between its radical left and more moderate wings. The Labor candidate, Michael Foot, contrasted sharply with Margaret Thatcher. He looked and acted like an absent-minded professor. Foot could talk for hours without reading from a prepared speech. But too often he rambled and lost his point. One columnist called him "a kind of walking obituary for the Labor Party."

Beyond his lack of skill and appeal as a campaigner, Foot had the additional problem of campaigning on the Labor Party platform. It called for pulling Great Britain out of the European Economic Community, banishing nuclear weapons from Britain, nationalizing a number of new industries, and spending $17 billion to create new jobs. To the great majority of the British population, each one of these was an extreme position.

In contrast, Margaret Thatcher appeared to be basking in her popularity. She presented the Conservative program flawlessly. She was, as usual, totally self-confident and aggressive. In a sense, her personality became the main issue in the campaign. This was reflected in the Conservative slogan, "The Resolute Approach."

On the major issues, the Conservatives took positions just the opposite of Labor's. Her new government, Thatcher insisted, would stay in the European Community. It would accept the new Pershing missiles to be deployed by the United States. And under no circumstances would it increase government spending. This, Thatcher insisted, would only bring about a new increase in inflation. Finally, rather than nationalizing more industries, the Conservatives intended to continue selling already nationalized companies, such as British Airways, to private investors.

When the votes were counted, Margaret Thatcher had won by the largest margin since the election of 1945. The Conservatives ended up with a majority of 144 seats over the combined opposition of the Labor Party and the Social Democratic/Liberal Alliance. At Conservative Party headquarters in London, with her husband Denis at her side, Thatcher told a happy crowd of her supporters, "It

May 16, 1983: Labor Party leader Michael Foot holds up a copy of his party's election manifesto. Many people thought Labor's 1983 proposals extreme, which accounted for the landslide victory gained by Thatcher and the Conservatives in June.

Mr. and Mrs. Thatcher cast their votes in the 1983 general election.

was a larger victory than I dared hope for."

Thatcher's modesty was somewhat misleading. During the campaign, she was well aware that she was riding the crest of her dramatic triumph in the Falkland Islands. She knew also that the opposition was weak, disorganized, and bumbling. She had every reason to believe that she would emerge a big winner—as she did.

Perhaps the poster held up by a smiling band of women in north London during the campaign said it best: "MAGGIE IS OUR MAN!"

8

Ten More Years

Soon after she was first elected prime minister in 1979, Margaret Thatcher told an interviewer that she would need about 10 years to "move this country in a new direction, to change the way we look at things, to create a wholly new attitude of mind." Initially it seemed unlikely that she would be prime minister long enough to achieve those ambitious goals, but Britain's 1982 victory in the Falklands War and Thatcher's subsequent triumph in the 1983 election gave her the chance to shape political life in her country for years to come.

Besides the Falklands factor, two significant economic achievements helped bring about the 1983 Tory landslide. First, the annual inflation rate had fallen from 20% to 4.6% during the 5 years of the Thatcher government; second, the power of the unions had been greatly curbed. Nevertheless, the British economy was still in very grave condition: Unemployment had tripled since 1979, industrial production had dropped 16%, and despite Thatcher's efforts to trim the budget, government spending remained as high as when she had first taken office.

In March 1984, with unemployment already at a post–World War II high of more than 13%, the Thatcher government announced that it would close 20 "unproductive" coal mines, a move that would put at least 20,000 miners out of work. The coal miners' union struck in protest, and within days more than 200,000 miners and dock workers

If Thatcher's policies are not changed, we can say goodbye to the British economy.
—SIR IAN GILMOUR
deputy foreign secretary in Thatcher's cabinet, after he was fired

"JOBS NOT BOMBS" is the message at this demonstration. Mrs. Thatcher's decision to buy expensive American Trident nuclear missiles for Britain's deterrent forces while cutting social programs was not popular with British left-wingers.

101

had walked off the job. The government refused to alter its plan, and when nonunion replacement laborers were hired, violence broke out on the picket lines. Strikers and police clashed, hundreds of miners were arrested, and Thatcher was criticized by opposition and Tory M.P.s alike for her "inept" and "insensitive" handling of the strike. Still, she did not budge; after 12 bitter months the union finally caved in and the miners returned to work — without having gained any concessions from the Thatcher government. Although this was counted as a victory for the Conservatives, most commentators agreed that the Thatcher program had left Britain's economy in a shambles.

Problems loomed on other fronts as well. Critics pointed out that the British garrison defending the Falklands was costing the financially strapped government billions. The Spanish government stepped up its demands for the return of the British colony of Gibraltar, located at Spain's southern tip and held by Britain since 1704. Closer to home, the Thatcher government's purchase of expensive nuclear cruise missiles from the United States sparked a number of protests from Britain's sizable disarmament and antinuclear movements, as well as from those who believed the government could ill afford to spend so much money on the weapons. But the biggest and most difficult problem of all involved the long crisis in Northern Ireland.

The British had occupied Ireland — often brutally — for hundreds of years until 1921, when the predominantly Catholic southern Ireland finally gained its independence from mainly Protestant Britain. However, six counties in the north of Ireland — a section of the country where two-thirds of the population is Protestant — voted to remain part of the United Kingdom, as Britain is officially called. The six counties became known as Northern Ireland, and they were granted parliamentary representation, like all other counties and metropolitan areas in the British Isles. In 1968–69 Catholics in Northern Ireland staged a series of demonstrations, charging that they were being discriminated against by the Protestant majority, who staged counter-demonstrations. Rioting broke out; shooting and bombing attacks by Catholic and Protestant terrorist groups soon followed. The British army was called in to restore order but instead was seen as an occupying force and itself became the target of rioters and paramilitary attacks. The local parliament was shut down and a form of martial law imposed, under which suspects could be jailed indefinitely without being brought to trial. By 1984 more than 2,000 people, most of them civilians, had been killed in sectarian violence in Northern Ireland; some 15,000 British troops were stationed there.

It was a crisis Thatcher had inherited when she became prime minister, but she was no more able to resolve it than were her predecessors. Her hardline policies in Northern Ireland brought her severe criticism from both Protestants and Catholics in Northern Ireland, moderates and leftists in Britain itself, Irish Catholics in Canada and the United States, and human rights organizations around the world, but she refused to withdraw the army or lift martial law. It nearly cost Thatcher her life.

On October 12, 1984, the annual Conservative Party Conference was being held at a large hotel in the southern seaside resort city of Brighton. Thatcher, her cabinet, most of the party's M.P.s and major local officials, and their families were there to spend the evening in preparation for Thatcher's appearance before the conference the next day. Security was tight, but somehow a bomb had been planted on the hotel's seventh floor.

At about 10:30 P.M. the bomb exploded with a deafening roar; the middle section of the building collapsed, floor caving in atop floor. Four people were killed and 32 hurt, but Thatcher escaped injury — she had left the bathroom of her second-floor suite just minutes before the blast sent a ton of debris crashing through the bathroom ceiling.

The Irish Republican Army, a secret paramilitary and terrorist group outlawed in both Ireland and Britain, claimed responsibility for the bombing. "Although we were unlucky this time," read the IRA statement, "we only have to be lucky once to suc-

Nuclear weapons and unemployment continue to dominate political debate in Britain. Many Britons feel that the prospects for life and work remain uncertain. Anti-nuclear demonstrations such as this continue in Britain to this day.

The "People's March for Jobs" proceeds through London, June 5, 1983. Even in the aftermath of Britain's victory in the Falklands, Mrs. Thatcher faced widespread opposition to her policies.

ceed." A few hours later, Thatcher told reporters that the bombing was the work of "evil men" who would not deter her, the party, or the government from continuing their duties. She went on as scheduled with her speech the next day, telling the conference and a national television and radio audience that "all attempts to destroy democracy by terrorism will fail."

In 1985, Northern Ireland was one of the areas suffering most from unemployment; Scotland and the north of England were also hard hit, and unemployment was blamed in part for a new round of rioting in the poorer sections of London and Birmingham. Public dissatisfaction with Thatcher and the Conservatives grew. Polls showed that Labor had drawn even with the Tories and that both were closely trailed by the Social Democratic–Liberal Alliance. Yet Thatcher remained confident that her monetarist policies and her dismantling of the British socialist state would succeed.

Then, in 1986, some sectors of the British economy turned around, spurred by the worldwide boom in financial markets, real estate, high-tech manufacturing, and retailing. The British middle and upper classes began to prosper, and while the industrial north continued to struggle under low income and high unemployment, London and the south made impressive economic gains. Overall the jobless rate in Britain declined; many credited the Thatcher program with the upturn. Thatcher herself hailed the gains as a vindication of her free-market policies. "Step by step," she said, "we are rolling back the frontiers of socialism and returning power to the people."

By now many saw Thatcher and her American counterpart, Ronald Reagan, as the standard bearers of a "conservative revolution" that was sweeping the Western democracies in the 1980s. Indeed, the British prime minister and the U.S. president maintained a close working relationship that was growing into a warm personal friendship; when American reporters asked Thatcher what she thought of Reagan, she replied, "I'm his biggest fan." The two leaders rarely disagreed publicly, but Thatcher was critical of the Reagan administration's policy of borrowing to fuel economic growth, a practice that led to the amassing of an enormous U.S. national debt.

Thatcher was widely respected for her foreign policy achievements. Soon after taking office in 1979 she had mediated a settlement in the long civil war in the former British colony of Rhodesia, formulating the transition in that African country (now called Zimbabwe) from a white-minority racist government to a democratically elected black-majority government. In 1984, she negotiated an agreement with China ensuring the peaceful return of the British colony of Hong Kong to that country in 1997. She had little choice in the matter — the British lease

Do people really want another four years of being lectured?
—quoted from an editorial in the *Spectator* magazine shortly before the 1983 election

Clutching a handful of paper money, a determined-looking Mrs. Thatcher prepares to speak in defense of her economic policies at a Conservative Party rally in 1983. The success of her attack on inflation inspired one British worker to declare: "I am better off today than I was just a few years ago."

on the wealthy colony was due to expire in 1997 anyway — but she was praised for gaining guarantees that Hong Kong would retain some self-government well into the 21st century. And despite Thatcher's staunchly anticommunist rhetoric, the Soviets admired the prime minister for her ability in arms control negotiations. When the reformer Mikhail Gorbachev became the leader of the Soviet Union in 1985, he and Thatcher had already established a strong mutual respect during meetings that had taken place during the previous two years.

Having scored recent economic and foreign-relations successes, a confident Thatcher announced in May 1987 that elections would be held the following month. The brief, hard-fought campaign centered on one overriding issue — whether voters should grant Thatcher and Thatcherism a third term at Britain's helm. When the results were in, they showed that the Tories had won in the south and the London suburbs — areas that had benefited from the economic upturn — while Labor had won in the still-depressed north and the inner cities. But it was enough for Thatcher; she and the Conservatives were victorious again, taking 42% of the total vote against Labor's 33% and the Social Democratic–Liberal Alliance's 23%. The Tories' 144-seat majority in the House of Commons was cut to a 101-seat margin, but it was still large enough to give Thatcher a free hand for several years to come.

Her opponents had warned that Thatcher was growing too powerful, that she was running roughshod over many British institutions — particularly the principle of free speech — and pointed to several events that occurred during her second term. In 1984, they pointed out, the Thatcher government had invoked the decades-old Official Secrets Act to jail civil servants who had leaked stories to British newspapers; in 1985 it banned a British Broadcasting Corporation documentary about Northern Ireland; in 1986 it stopped publication of a book about British military intelligence in the 1950s; and in 1987 it ordered police to raid the BBC's Scottish offices and confiscate all material pertaining to a documentary about a British spy satellite. Thatcher's critics at home were joined by American free-press advocates in 1988, when her government censored a retired English officer's memoirs about his experiences as a British spy in the 1950s, and in 1989, when it tried to censor a Thames Television documentary about the killing of two suspected IRA gunmen. Several prominent British writers and publishing figures, deploring Thatcher's frequent efforts to silence authors, publishers, and journalists, called for Britain to adopt a U.S.-style bill of rights guaranteeing freedom of the press. Thatcher rejected the idea, saying that the nation's security was more important.

In early 1989, Thatcher made one of her boldest moves yet, in what many saw as an attack on a cornerstone of British life — the National Health Service. The National Health, as most Britons call it, had been founded in 1948 to ensure every resident of the nation free health and hospital care; the system was admired the world over for its fairness and its efficiency. Nevertheless, it cost the government money, and — perhaps for Thatcher its worst offense — it was a socialist program. She proposed giving hospitals the option of withdrawing from the public system and becoming private, profit-seeking institutions instead. Thatcher's critics were appalled. Social Democratic Party leader David Owen, himself a physician, said Thatcher's proposal threatened to make Britain's model health-care system more like that of the United States, where there was "first-rate treatment for the wealthy and 10th-rate treatment for the poor."

However vocal her critics, by the end of the 1980s, Margaret Thatcher was indisputably recognized as one of the most powerful and influential prime ministers Britain had ever had. She had served for more than a decade, and, guided by her conservative philosophy, tried tirelessly to lead Britain out of near bankruptcy and back into the world's first rank of nations. Her tenure has been without question highly controversial, but it is equally clear that Thatcher has been guided by her conscience. "All power is trust," she once said. "We have to use our power wisely and well."

> *Things will get worse before they get better.*
> —MARGARET THATCHER
> after becoming prime
> minister in 1979

Further Reading

Arnold, Bruce. *Margaret Thatcher: A Study in Power.* London: Hannish Hamilton, 1984.

Beer, Samuel H. *Modern British Politics.* New York: Norton, 1982.

Bruce-Gardyne, Jock. *Mrs. Thatcher's First Administration: The Prophets Confounded.* London: Macmillan, 1984.

Calvocoressi, Peter. *The British Experience 1945–75.* New York: Pantheon, 1978.

Gamble, Andrew. *Britain in Decline.* Boston: Beacon Press, 1981.

Gardiner, George. *Margaret Thatcher: From Childhood to Leadership.* London: Kimber, 1975.

Holmes, Martin. *The First Thatcher Government, 1979–1983: Contemporary Conservatism and Economic Change.* Brighton, Sussex: Wheatsheaf Books, 1985.

Jones, Margaret. *Thatcher's Kingdom: A View of Britain in the Eighties.* Sydney: Collins, 1984.

Junor, Penny. *Margaret Thatcher: Wife, Mother, Politician.* London: Sidgwick & Jackson, 1983.

Kavanaugh, Dennis. *Thatcherism and British Politics: The End of Consensus?* New York: Oxford University Press, 1987.

Krieger, Joel. *Reagan, Thatcher, and the Politics of Decline.* Cambridge, England: Polity Press, 1986.

Lewis, Russel. *Margaret Thatcher: A Personal and Political Biography.* Boston: Routledge & Kegan Paul, 1984.

Mayer, Allan J. *Britain's First Lady: Margaret Thatcher and Her Rise to Power.* New York: Newsweek Books, 1979.

Minogue, Kenneth, and Michael Biddess, eds. *Thatcherism: Personality and Politics.* London: Macmillan, 1987.

Money, Ernie. *Margaret Thatcher.* London: International Publications Service, 1976.

Riddell, Peter. *The Thatcher Government.* Oxford: M. Robertson, 1983.

Sampson, Anthony. *The Changing Anatomy of Britain.* New York: Random House, 1983.

Stewart, Michael. *Politics and Economic Policy in the United Kingdom Since 1964; The Jekyll and Hyde Years.* London: Pergamon, 1978.

Thatcher, Carol. *Diary of an Election: With Margaret Thatcher on the Campaign Trail.* London: Sidgwick & Jackson, 1983.

Chronology

Oct. 13, 1926	Born Margaret Hilda Roberts in Grantham, England
1947	Graduates from Oxford University
1951	Marries Denis Thatcher
1954	Admitted to the bar
1959	Elected to Parliament, representing London suburb of Finchley
1967	Chosen for shadow cabinet
1969	Shadow minister of education
1970	Minister of education in Heath government
1975	Elected leader of Conservative Party
May 1979	Elected prime minister
1981	High unemployment sparks widespread inner-city rioting
April 1982	Argentina invades Falkland Islands
June 1982	Britain recaptures Falklands; 1,000 Argentinians and 255 Britons killed
June 1983	Thatcher elected to second term as prime minister
March 1984	Coal miners begin 12-month strike
Oct. 12, 1984	Irish Republican Army bomb kills four at Conservative Party Conference in Brighton; Thatcher escapes injury
1986	British economy rallies, unemployment falls
June 1987	Thatcher elected to third term as prime minister
1988	Steps up efforts to censor books, newspapers, and magazines
1989	Announces program to begin privatization of National Health Service

Index

PICTURE CREDITS

Wide World Photos: pp. 2, 14, 16, 17, 18, 19, 20, 21, 24, 25, 26, 28, 29, 32, 35, 36, 38, 39, 40, 41, 42, 43, 44, 46, 48, 49, 50, 51, 52, 53, 54, 55, 57, 58, 61, 62, 63, 65, 67, 68–69, 70, 71, 74, 75, 76, 77, 78, 79, 80, 81, 82, 83, 85, 87, 88, 89, 91, 92, 93, 95, 96, 98, 99, 100, 101, 102, 104, 107, 108

Bernard Garfinkel is a writer and editor who lives in New York City. A graduate of the University of Missouri with a Master's degree in history, he also studied at Columbia University.

His articles have appeared in numerous national magazines, including *True* and *Gentleman's Quarterly.* He is the author (with Jules Siegel) of *The Journal of the Absurd* and of several children's books, including *The Champions, Call to Glory,* and *My Growing Up Book.*

Arthur M. Schlesinger, jr. taught history at Harvard for many years and is currently Albert Schweitzer Professor of the Humanities at City University of New York. He is the author of numerous highly praised works in American history and has twice been awarded the Pulitzer Prize. He served in the White House as special assistant to Presidents Kennedy and Johnson.